SHORT CU

INTRODUCTIONS TO FILM STUDIES

OTHER TITLES IN THE SHORT CUTS SERIES

TRASH CINEMA

THE LURE OF THE LOW

GUY BAREFOOT

WALLFLOWER
LONDON and NEW YORK

A Wallflower Press book
Published by
Columbia University Press
Publishers Since 1893
New York • Chichester, West Sussex
cup.columbia.edu

Wallflower Press® is a registered trademark of Columbia University Press.

Cataloging-in-Publication Data available from the Library of Congress.

ISBN 978-0-231-18037-5 (pbk. : alk. paper)
ISBN 978-0-231-54269-2 (e-book)

Columbia University Press books are printed on permanent and durable acid-free paper.

Printed in the United States of America

Cover image: GLEN OR GLENDA (1953) © Screen Classics

CONTENTS

ACKNOWLEDGEMENTS

My thanks to Yoram Allon, Commissioning Editor at Wallflower Press, for his patience. Thanks also to James Chapman, Claire Jenkins and Gozde Naiboglu at the University of Leicester, and to members of the School of Arts Film Research Group. Others who have helped me include I. Q. Hunter, Iain Robert Smith and the staff at the British Film Institute's Reuben Library. Thanks also to Sara Barefoot for helping me keep going.

1   DEFINITIONS AND DEBATES

On 13 October 2015, Synapse Films released a newly restored version of *Manos: The Hands of Fate* on Blu-ray and DVD. Special features included audio commentaries by two of the actors, a trio of featurettes – 'Hands: The Fate of Manos', 'Restoring the Hands of Manos', 'Felt: The Puppet Hands of Fate' (a puppet version of the original film) – and an unrestored version of the film. A novelisation was published the following month, when Ship to Store Media also released 'the definitive audio edition of MANOS: The Hands of Fate'. *Growing Up with Manos: The Hands of Fate: How I Was the Child Star of the Worst Movie Ever Made and Lived to Tell the Tale*, written by Jackie Newman Jones ('Debbie' in the film), followed in early 2016. *Manos Returns* is in post-production at the time of writing.

The film restoration had been a labour of love, supported by crowd funding, that went back to 2011. *Manos* had received its original premiere in at the Capri Theatre, El Paso, Texas, on 15 November 1966. Emerson Releasing Corporation subsequently gave it a limited, drive-in run. It achieved wider recognition after 30 January 1993, when (not for the last time) it was featured on *Mystery Science Theater 3000*, accompanied by Tom Servo and Crow T. Robot's running commentary on the film. Rhino Home Video released that version on DVD in 2001 as well as a DVD with *Santa Claus Conquers the Martians* (1964) in 2004, while the 2003 Alpha Video release came without the *Mystery Science Theater* riffs. Shout! Factory issued *Manos: The Hands of Fate: Special Edition* in 2011. The two-disc package included the 2001 version along the unrestored print and a documentary, *Hotel Torgo*.

The work in progress restoration was screened in 2012. The website dedicated to the project pointed out that this was 'a matter of feet from where the film had premiered 46 years ago'; one of those who had attended the 'legendary original screening' commented that the 'restoration, even unfinished, was looking better than the film ever had in its original release' (Solover 2012). There were further screenings in Los Angeles, New York, Montreal and non-American locations such as Copenhagen, Helsinki and Tartu, Estonia. In the words of the Synapse press release:

> MANOS: THE HANDS OF FATE, the sole directorial effort of Texas fertilizer salesman Harold P. Warren, perplexed even the most jaded Drive-In audiences and was deemed by many 'the worst movie ever made'. Nearly lost, the original 16mm Ektachrome film elements have been finally unearthed and lovingly restored by Ben Solover...
> (Solover 2015)

Why? Why all this attention, even devotion, to a film notable for its failure? For a start, the title is absurd: translating *manos* as 'hands' leaves 'Hands: The Hands of Fate'. There is a story, about a lost couple, their child and dog, encountering a satyr, Torgo, the mysterious Master, and the Master's six imprisoned wives, but the way in which it is told is fragmented and often incoherent. Sequences unconnected to the main narrative (notably shots of a courting couple in a car in the middle of nowhere) are repeated without discernible purpose. Much of the early part of the film is taken up with Torgo taking the visitors' luggage out of their car, then putting it back, then taking it out again. Performances are awkward, and hindered by the dubbing and dialogue that is as repetitive as the action and spaced out between insignificant pauses. Horror gets little further than the wives trying to do scary things with their hands. The editing is hopelessly fragmented. The central location is introduced without an establishing shot while close-ups that might have served as reaction shots become meaningless in the absence of any visible subject of their reaction. Torgo's identity as a satyr is never actually clarified and his disappearance from the final section is never explained. The cool jazz soundtrack is an interesting touch and might have worked well in another context but feels awkwardly incongruous in a supposed horror film.

My question is not merely rhetorical. There are different possible explanations for the longevity of *Manos*, little seen immediately after its completion but subsequently retaining a much higher visibility than other films of its time, and an enduring presence among the IMDb's 'bottom 100' list. Most obviously, it appeals on the 'so bad it is good' principle, offering entertainment because of its failings. I. Q. Hunter identifies it as not just a 'bad film' but a 'badfilm', a film where badness 'is not a mere summary of critical disapproval but denotes a complete abrogation of the minimum standards of filmmaking' (2014: 487). The badfilm here is 'perhaps the purest kind of trash cinema' and *Manos* is 'a truly canonical Badfilm' (ibid.)

The film has its defenders. In the other book called *Trash Cinema* (sub-title: *A Celebration of Overlooked Masterpieces*), Rob Craig discusses the film's uncanniness and bleak minimalism and argues that it reflects 'profound socio-cultural forces abounding in the world at the time', standing 'almost as a bizarre ritualistic destruction of the postwar American family, and its replacement by a bleak, amoral hippie commune, replete with torture, sexual perversion and hints of totalitarianism (2015: 139, 140). But bad films can be seen as important without such claims. For Ian Olney, the bad film's popularity can be explained by the possibilities it offers for 'performative spectatorship'; in celebrating failure, fans use such films as a way of establishing individual identity and a sense of community (2013: 78–9). Hunter points out that the film is readable in ways that more competent or guarded films are not, an insight into the maker's fantasies of middle-aged male control over beautiful young women. More generally, bad horror films, 'enable conditions for a kind of automatic filmmaking or at any rate can be gratefully appropriated as such for the style of excessive overinterpretation that cultists and academic fans value' (2014: 488). This can explain not only Craig's reading but also *Manos* as uncanny even in its hypnotic dullness, so that its absolute failure as a horror film is transformed 'into an inadvertent triumph of counter-cinema' (2014: 489).

Such cult celebrations depend on the film but also the extra-textual, and the myth surrounding the film. Torgo's satyr identity is not readable through the film alone (that is one of its failings), and the appearance of John Reynolds in the role is made genuinely poignant by the knowledge that he killed himself shortly before the film's release. Beyond that, the purchaser of the Synapse video was not merely getting an awkwardly made film but buying into a story of a Texas fertilizer salesman who made a bet about how cheaply he could make a film, about tired actors with day jobs forced to work with an incomplete script, and a failure so thorough it stretched to an inability to include a copyright notice on the film. The story in the film may have been dull but the story of the film approaches Texas noir.

All this was made possible by the film's survival and accessibility. It was because it was shown without a copyright notice at that legendary, 1966 El Paso screening that *Manos* passed immediately into the public domain, was then picked by television, and became available for *Mystery Science Theater* entertainment, later for wider fame. Trash is something we throw away but as I have discovered in researching this book, one of the most striking things about trash cinema is the extent to which it has survived and returned to view through changes in how films are circulated and watched as well as broader cultural shifts. The pervasiveness of low culture has been evident for a while. It was in 1995 that Jeffrey Sconce noted: 'Art museums that once programmed only Italian neo-Realism or German neo-Expressionism now feature retrospectives of 1960s Biker films and career overviews of exploitation auteurs such as Hershell Gordon Lewis and Doris Wishman ... academic courses in film studies increasingly investigate "sleazy" genres such as horror and pornography' (1995: 373). Trash cinema can seem like a case-book example of the return of the repressed, as films buried by disapproval and neglect come back to haunt us.

Sconce's article itself inspired debate and the expansion of trash as a strand of film studies. Returning to the topic in the following decade he discussed the rise of 'cine-cynicism' searching for a new critical language to discuss Hollywood flops such as *Gigli* (2003) and *Catwoman* (2004), and pointed that 'the entire oeuvre of Doris Wishman is now available on DVD while John Ford's is not' (2007a: 2). The same year saw the release of Quentin Tarantino and Robert Rodriguez's *Grindhouse* (2007), followed by a series of 'retrosploitation' films that also attempted to recreate the distressed look of a once despised part of cinema history. Otherwise what has changed is the increased availability of a culture once restricted to a limited circle of aficionados, as horror zines and paperback books have made way for a plethora of blogs, forums and online videos. What were once the most obscure films are now available through a click on a screen, whether in the form of high-definition restorations or grainy online download from the public domain or somewhere close to that.

Trash has resurfaced in different forms. As I write, the Criterion Collection, specialist in high-quality reissues of 'important classic and contemporary films', has just brought out the restored version of *Multiple Maniacs* (1970) on Blu-ray, John Waters' 'gloriously grotesque second feature', complete with accompanying essays (including Linda Yablonsky's 'Genuine Trash'), a documentary, interviews and the director's audio commentary. The September 2015 issue of *Sight & Sound* included not only an interview with Waters ('John Waters Talks Trash') but articles from Tim Lucas and I. Q. Hunter on trash cinema. The 2016 highlights at London's Barbican Centre included 'Cheap Thrills: Trash, Movies and the Art of Transgression'. More regular events include Breda's BUT (B-movie, Underground and Trash) Film Festival ('"Trash films" are over the top films in content and imagery', explains the website), the Trash Film Festival in Varazdin, Croatia, showing 'action movies, horrors and SciFi epics – and the common property of them all is exaggeration in the given genre characteristic', the Trash Film Festival in Berlin, which in 2015 emphasised its 'Ironic-Action-Horror-Fantasy short film festival and more', and Barcelona's Horrorvision Festival, pitching itself more specifically as the 'Spanish Horror-Trash Film Festival'.

Asking about the appeal of trash cinema, and thinking about the reasons for studying it, of course involves asking *what* as well as *why*. A film such as *Manos* can suggest trash as bad. Today 'Bad Film Clubs' screen films such as *The Room* (2003) while internet lists of worst movies abound. This celebration is nothing new. *Harvard Lampoon* began producing annual 'worst of...' film awards in 1940, a tradition continued from 1980 by running the Golden Raspberry Awards at the same time as the Academy Awards. American television had been broadcasting films on account of, rather than despite, their perceived shortcomings since the 1950s, a tradition picked up in 1988 when *Mystery Science Theater 3000* began broadcasting cheap genre films as part of a comedy routine. The Medved brothers' *The Fifty Worst Movies of All Time* (1979), *The Golden Turkey Awards* (1980) and *The Son of Golden Turkey Awards* (1986) led in 1983 to the UK's Channel 4 series, *The Worst of Hollywood*.

This badness has been characterised in different ways. Edward Margulies and Stephen Rebello introduced their *Bad Movies We Love* not as cheap trash but as films 'that separate themselves from the pack, special Bad Movies: those big-budget, big-star, big-director, aggressively publicized fiascos that have gone wonderfully, irredeemably, lovably haywire' (1983: xvii). In justifying the publication of *The Fifty Worst Movies of All Time* on the grounds that 'people show greater enthusiasm in laughing together over films they despise than in trying to praise the films they admire' (1978: 9), Harry Medved and his co-authors positioned themselves as defenders of established values. J. Hoberman allowed that the Medveds' publications and performances could have a levelling effect, deflating seriousness and identifying Hollywood fallibility, but his 1980 essay on 'Bad Movies' explored the bad further, from the surrealist 'Learn to go see the "worst" films; they are sometimes sublime' to Jack Smith's obsession with the 'bad acting' of Maria Montez; 'bad' here leads to either the surrealist marvellous or truthfulness, Montez films as 'unintended documentaries of a romantic, narcissistic young woman dressing up in pasty jewels, striking fantastic poses, queening it over an all-too-obviously make-believe world' (1991: 14).

For Hoberman, films such as Edward D. Wood's Jr's *The Bride of the Monster* (1956) were 'objectively bad'. The criteria here is failure as well as lack of quality, *The Bride of the Monster* as a film that aspired to Hollywood standards but failed miserably. Yet he identified subjectivity as another reason for writing about bad movies, the reason being that 'tastes change; that many, if not most, of the films we admire were once dismissed as inconsequential trash' (1991: 13).

Tastes not only change but differ. 'The favourite picture in France today', wrote Harry Potamkin in 1933, 'the favourite artistic picture, is generally an American one, and what we consider here trash, aesthetically or ethically reprehensible, will be exhibited in Paris as art' (1933: 5). He was discussing the French response to *A Girl in Every Port* (1928), directed by Howard Hawks with a cast including Louise Brooks. Both Hawks and Brooks have gone on to be celebrated in America as well as France: their elevated status in no longer controversial. The celebration of trash cinema here exists in a tradition of cinephilia, auteur theory, the analysis of *Dumb and Dumber* (1994) in the light of *Don Quixote* (1605–1615) (see Simon 1999: 4) and the broader understanding of cinema as an important art form (but not just in its art cinema form), approaching it seriously or at least treasuring it in some way.

A more precise understanding of trash cinema has been as a sub-genre, a particular form of exploitation film that properly emerged in the 1970s and has been particularly associated with that decade and the one that immediately followed. At the beginning of his *British Trash Cinema*, I. Q. Hunter explains that he uses 'trash' first to refer 'straightforwardly enough, to exploitation films – low-budget genre movies, mostly, which have sometimes gained cult reputations for their oddness and rarity', though he extends the term to include 'straightforwardly "bad" films like *Raise the Titanic* (1980)' and 'what is usually dismissed as rubbishy hack-work, like *Dirty Weekend* (1993) and *Outlaw* (2007)' (2013: viii). An advantage of this approach lies in its use of trash less as a judgement than as a label, within which it is possible to explore films rather than simply dismiss them. Thus, to take an even narrower category, between 1988 and 1998 the *European Trash Cinema* zine concentrated on horror films from continental Europe, mainly Italy, not as failures but out of enthusiasm for this strand of cinema as a whole, and in order to promote and assess individual examples. In 2014, zine founder Craig Ledbetter went on to set up a 'European Trash Cinema' blog, which he introduced thus:

> Welcome to a blog about the trashy side of European Cinema. When I created the magazine EUROPEAN TRASH CINEMA back in 1988, it received heavy criticism for using the term "TRASH" in regards to films. Well, the dumb asses never figured out I was being IRONIC when I used eurotrash. I was laughing at all the critics and snobs who thumbed their noses at genre cinema. ('Ledster' 2014)

The irony here is designed at the expense of the critics rather than the films. A similar comment can be found in Max Allan Collins' introduction to a collection of reviews published as *Asian Cult Cinema*. Collins described how, having published reviews of Hong Kong action films in the fanzine, *Naked! Screaming! Terror!* in 1991, Thomas Weisser continued this work in this new publication (see Collins 1997: 2). However, notes Collins, invoking 'trash' was not to be taken too seriously: 'the hard-core, cult-movie audience ... was well-aware that Weisser's tongue was in cheek. By using "trash" he invoked snobby movie critics dismissing any genre fare as beneath contempt. ... In fact, the Hong Kong cinema discovered by Weisser and a handful of others ... has more than its share of treasures among the trash' (ibid.).. The difference here is that Ledbetter continued to define his interest as in 'the trashy side of European cinema'. The Asian 'treasures among the trash' evidently warranted changing the name from *Asian Trash Cinema* to *Asian Cult Cinema*, even though the book version was still published by ATC/ETC publications, that is, Asian Trash Cinema/ European Trash Cinema.

The term 'Eurotrash' itself illustrates a shifting vocabulary. It emerged in early 1980s New York. It was initially a derogatory term for wealthy European immigrants, a xenophobic variation on the class and racial dismissal of the 'white trash' label (see Hogrefe 1984). By the end of the decade Ledbetter was putting the term to different use in his zines (with Eurotrash as part of the vocabulary at least in 1989) while in the 1990s it was being applied more generally to, as a *Guardian* fashion report put it, 'the too blond, too thin, just rich enough Euro-trash' (Chunn 1990: 46) who were the market for Italian designers. Its adoption in 1993 for the British Channel 4 programme, *Eurotrash*, combined this fashion image with connotations of 'trash TV' (for which the earliest use given by the *Oxford English Dictionary* is from 1985). Reporting on the forthcoming show for the *Washington Post*, Peter Mikelbank quoted co-host Jean-Paul Gaultier (described as 'the fashion designer who brought high fashion to fabulous new lows) as saying, 'I love kitschy, trashy, tacky things... So I am not insulted when people call me "Trash". I use a lot of trash after all for my inspiration. And, anyway, we are all trash to someone' (1993: F1). The same article quoted co-host Antoine de Gaunes on the existence of 'an internationally developed trash culture originating in the U.S. and Europe, mixing, crossbreeding trash attitudes without distinction. It began with punks, with Gaultier impertinence, his rupture with the traditional French fashion industry and the attitudes they represented' (ibid.). In the 1970s Mario Bava's *Lisa and the Devil* (1972) was adapted for the American market under the title *House of Exorcism* and distributed through 'underbelly runs', playing as a support title 'in drive-ins and innercity grind houses alongside kung-fu films, blaxploitation pictures, and midnight horror screenings' (Heffernan 2007: 158); thus the film became 'simply another example of "Eurotrash" – inexpensively mounted genre pictures, usually co-productions between two or more European studios featuring down-at-the-heels American players in roles designed to capitalize on hits from major Hollywood studios' (ibid.). In this account, it was only after the 1980s/90s critical reappraisal of filmmakers working in lowbrow forms that Bava's masterpiece was able to re-emerge from the shadow of Eurotrash (see Heffernan 2007: 159–60). An alternative strategy has been to invoke trash to emphasise the inter-relationship between the highbrow and the lowbrow. In Joan Hawkins' 'Sleaze Mania, Euro-Trash and High Art: The Place of European Art Films in American Low Culture' (1999) trash seems to link the European high and the American low. In *Alternative Europe: Eurotrash and Exploitation Cinema Since 1945* (Mathijs and Mendik 2004) it is used to signify excess and the extreme, from nazis-ploitation cinema to Jorg Buttgereit's *Nekromantik* (1987), but also the avant-garde. Trash here is nasty rather than just bad.

Garbage and Garbology

The more material sense of trash has itself become the subject of study within the wider field of garbology. The paradoxical importance of what is discarded is one reason why it has attracted increasing attention. The 'social science of garbage' is based on the premise that

> What we classify and dispose of as waste provides rich insight into our behaviour, social structures, and treatment of our envi-ronment. ... Archaeologists have long studied artefacts of refuge from a distant past as a portal into ancient civilizations lacking written testaments, but examining what we throw away today tells a story in real time and becomes an important and useful tool for academic study. Our trash is a testament; what we throw away says much about our values, our habits, and our lives (Zimring 2012: xxv)

Thus, a further reason for paying attention to trash cinema may not be because it is either bad or good but because films lower down the scale may be more revealing, in the sense that they are unguarded but also closer to the world in which we live. Trash cinema has particular documentary value. As one writer put it: 'We may aspire to the shining *heroics* of Steven Spielberg or the existential angst of Woody Allen, but as long as there is dacron, linoleum, and velvet Mediterranean furniture our lives are best left interpreted by Larry Buchanan' (Goodsell 1988: 31). Buchanan's oeuvre includes films such as *Zontar, The Thing from Venus* (1966), a slavish and impoverished remake of *It Conquered the World* (1956), itself a quickly-produced science fiction film for the drive-ins and the teens.

This wider study of trash has developed in different ways. Michael Thompson's 'rubbish theory' (1979) was developed out of a study of how different items of durable (increasing) value moved from transient (decreasing) value through rubbish (no value). That is, value is unstable rather than intrinsic, a response to social pressure, and things can take on greater value precisely because they were once judged worthless.

Trash took on particular significance in a consumer society, and critiques of that society could complain about what was seen as its disposable culture along with the physical objects that were designed for obsolesce. However, even culture industry critiques left room for a focus on trash, junk, garbage, waste (a recurring modernist trope) or refuse. Garbage (*Müll*) meant different things to Theodor Adorno. Sarah Edith James interprets his condemnation of all post-Auschwitz culture as garbage as meaning that the sphere of 'resurrected culture' (that which he saw as merely rehashing traditional values of truth, beauty, and goodness, as if the Holocaust had never happened) should be considered as mere refuse' (2012: 4). Yet his criticism of the logic of capitalist production was based on the belief that it relegated to the junk pile everything not in line with the most recent methods of industrial production. On this basis he 'suggested that people should address the "waste products" and "blind spots" of history so as to reclaim their radical potential' (2012: 5). Describing the method of his Arcades Project as 'literary montage' Adorno's associate Walter Benjamin wrote of his interest in 'the rags, the refuse', and the 'Refuse of History' (1999: 460, 461). As Marita Bullock notes, later critics picked up on 'Benjamin's writings on the trash of history', identifying him 'as a precursor to the postmodern claim that history is not the seamless, objective, teleological tranche of time that it claims to be, but ... a stockpile of forgotten junk and detritus that can be reconfigured in the image of those forgotten or trampled by the victors of history' (2012: 35).

The metaphor of trash and garbage has been appropriated for cinema on an international level. The Brazilian Cinema da Boca do Lixo ('Mouth of Garbage' film) takes its name from the Boca do Lixo region of San Paulo, but in addition, notes Robert Stam, 'For the underground filmmakers, the garbage metaphor captured the sense of marginality, of being condemned to survive within scarcity, of being the dumping ground for transnational capitalism, of being obliged to recycle the materials of the dominant culture' (1997: 284). Applying this to African cinema, Kenneth Harrow argues that

> trash, above all, refers to people who have been dismissed from the community, marginalized and forgotten, turned into 'bare lives' in 'states of exception' for others to study and pity. Trash encompasses the turning of that reduced status into the basis for revolt, change, and the turning away from regimes that produce definitions of trash to newly formulated regimes that force us to reconsider the criteria for assigning value. (2013: x)

Trash is global. The *Oxford English Dictionary* traces its English roots back to the sixteenth century, and before cinema the word had been established as a dismissive term for popular culture. When, on 31 December 1875, the *Manchester Guardian* reported on a boy sentenced for two months hard labour for stealing £8 it noted that, 'He admitted that he had been reading "periodicals of the Dick Turpin sort"', under the heading 'A RESULT OF READING TRASH'. Trash was thus neither twentieth century nor American in origin and has come to be identified in Nollywood as well as Hollywood but has taken on particular connotations in a modern world dominated by American mass culture in general.

Cultural commentators have often worried about this, but under different names. In 'The Avant-Garde and Kitsch', Clement Greenberg defined, and condemned, kitsch as 'popular, commercial art and literature with their chromeotypes, magazine covers, illustrations, ads, slick and pulp fiction, comics, Tin Pan Alley music, tap dancing, Hollywood movies, etc. etc.' (1939: 39). The contrast Greenberg made between the avant-garde and kitsch was based on the notion that kitsch, a product of the industrial revolution, had displaced folk culture with ersatz culture, a culture 'destined for those who, insensible to the values of genuine culture, are hungry nevertheless for the diversion that only culture of some sort can provide' (ibid.). Modifying Greenberg's ideas, Dwight MacDonald distinguished between High Culture, Masscult and Midcult. For him, Masscult ranged from 'servant-girl romances' to radio, television and the movies ('almost entirely Masscult') (1962: 3). While Folk Art had its own authentic quality, Masscult was 'at best a vulgarised reflection of High Culture' (1962: 34). The hybrid Midcult pretended 'to respect the standards of High Culture while in fact it waters them down and vulgarises them' (1962: 37). It was 'the Museum of Modern Art's film department paying tribute to Samuel Goldwyn because his movies are alleged to be (slightly) better than those of other Hollywood producers – though why they are called "producers" when their function is to prevent the production of art (cf., the fate in Hollywood of Griffith, Chaplin, von Stroheim, Eisenstein and Orson Welles) is a semantic puzzle' (1962: 38). Both Masscult and its recent offspring Midcult represented 'a debased, trivial culture that avoids both the deep realities (sex, death, failure, tragedy) and also the simple, spontaneous pleasures' (1962: 71). From this perspective cinema in general was dominated by Masscult and Midcult, and was therefore trash.

However, when Steven L. Hamelman declared that 'American culture is trash culture' it was not a complaint (2004: 3). The statement comes at the beginning of his study of rock music and trash: others identified trash in the movies. In 'Trash, Art and the Movies', Pauline Kael argued that 'movies took their impetus not from the desiccated imitation European high culture, but from the peep show, the Wild West Show, the music hall, the comic strip – from what was coarse and common' (1970: 103). For Kael, trash lay at the heart of cinema, or at least of 'the movies', that popular/commercial strand of cinema particularly associated with Hollywood that some distinguish from the respectability of 'the film'. It was essential to the appeal of a crudely-made drama such as *Wild in the Streets* (1968) as well as slicker productions like *The Thomas Crown Affair* (1968). The latter was 'pretty good trash' (1970: 112), and 'seeing trash can liberate the spectator' (1970: 115) for its playful qualities. Kael's argument was both positive and purposely limiting. She argued that the appeal 'of movies is that we don't have to take them too seriously' (1970: 91), an argument she used against those alarmed at the effects of Hollywood movies but also those who 'try and place trash within an acceptable academic tradition' (1970: 112) (as I have been doing so far).

A Most Elastic Textual Category

Trash, then, is worth examining because it exists as part of a debate about our responses to films, from Kael's fears about taking trash too seriously to the link Jeffrey Sconce makes for 'the ongoing centrality of low cinema in all strata of film culture' and 'the continued vibrancy of film studies itself as a diverse and diversifying disciple' (2007: 4). It has been seen as a core element of popular cinema and as a specific if often imprecisely defined kind of film, but it resists precise definition.

Trash is often identified as part of a longer list. The *Videohound Guide to Cult Flics and Trash Pics* begins thus:

> For this book, we've culled what we term the 'Mongrel Video' – the masterpieces, the misfits and the misunderstood. We wanted to give special attention to cult movies, trash film, underground flicks, alternative cinema, and camp outings – movies so bad they're good, as well as movies so bad we don't want you to think they might have some camp value, and movies so good the cool people watch them over and over again. (Schwartz 1996: ix)

'*Psychotronic* films range from sincere social commentary to degrading trash', explained Michael Weldon at the beginning of *The Psychotronic Encyclopedia of Film* (1989: xii). In his introduction to an annotated bibliography on the exploitation film, Ernest Mathijs notes that 'the term "exploitation" is not uncontested. Terms such as "grindhouse", "trash", or "cult" (or "cinema bis" in French) are often used to denote (largely) the same films' (2011). In her discussion of 'the masculinity of cult' (see below), Joanne Hollows cites Cinebizarre's catalogue of 'Art films, Cult Film, Avant-Garde film, Giallobizarre, Hong Kong cinema, International Erotica, Midnight Movies, Exploitation and Sexploitation, gory Horror, sexy vampires, classic science fiction, European sex comedies, shock films and drive-in trash' (2003: 38). Perhaps most famously, in 'Trashing the Academy', Sconce defined 'paracinema' as 'a most elastic textual category', including

> such seemingly disparate subgenres as 'bad film', splatterpunk, 'mondo' films, sword and sandal epics, Elvis flicks, government

hygiene films, Japanese monster movies, beach-party musicals, and just about every manifestation of exploitation film from juvenile delinquency films to soft-core pornography. Paracinema is thus less a distinct group of films than a particular reading protocol, a counter-aesthetic turned sub-cultural sensibility devoted to all manner of cultural detritus. In short, the explicit manifesto of paracinematic culture is to valorize all forms of cinematic 'trash', whether such films have been explicitly rejected or simply ignored by legitimate film culture. (1995: 372)

In these different lists trash is either an item on a menu, a synonym, an umbrella term or one part of the broader umbrella of cult cinema. It appears within and without quotation marks.

Cult does not necessarily mean trash. When Daniel Peary included titles such as *Citizen Kane* (1941), *The Red Shoes* (1948) and *Singin' in the Rain* (1952) in his first book on *Cult Movies* (1982) it was not as representatives of trash cinema (as was suggested in his subtitle, '*The Classics, the Sleepers, the Weird and the Wonderful*'). However, there has been a tendency to understand cult cinema in terms of films dismissed by others as trash. Joanne Hollows' observation (quoting Barbara Klinger on collecting in the post-video era) that it was the '"low-end" cult based around "obscure and trashy titles" … that is most commonly employed by cult film media, distributors and retailers, and which has also preoccupied academic writing' (2003: 38) was born out by the appearance of her comments in a collection entitled *Defining Cult Movies* alongside other contributions on Spanish horror, and the exploitation and horror films of Dwain Esper, Peter Jackson, David Cronenberg, Dario Argento and Doris Wishman.

For Ernest Mathijs and Jamie Sexton, cult cinema is 'a kind of cinema identified by remarkably unusual audience receptions that stress the phenomenal component of the viewing experience, that upset traditional viewing strategies, that are situated at the margin of the mainstream, and that display reception tactics that have become a synonym for an attitude of minority resistance and niche celebration within mass culture' (2011: 8). They discuss 'Classical Hollywood Cults' but also 'Exploitation and B movies' (2011: 145–54), and, within that, 'Nasty Trash' (2011: 150–2). If cult therefore does not necessarily mean trash, does trash necessarily mean cult?

There has certainly been a tendency to discuss trash cinema in the context of cult, and Sconce's understanding of paracinema as 'a reading protocol, a counter-aesthetic turned sub-cultural sensibility devoted to all manner of cultural detritus', suggests the upsetting of traditional viewing strategies, marginal and minority resistance and niche celebration within mass culture. In I. Q. Hunter's words, 'By the 1970s "trash film" had hardened into a recognisable category of deliberately trashy movies catering to cultists delighting in bad taste, violence, kitsch, camp and sexual explicitness' (2013: 22). However, when Hunter moves on to 'British cult cinema' he comments, 'Not all cult films are trash, and not all trash is cult. … And though the *field* of British trash is very "culty" indeed, few *individual* British trash films will ever be, or deserve to be, cult favourites' (2013: 26).

Other key recurring terms are camp, kitsch and schlock, the latter two linked together by Charles Flynn (1975) when he set the 'schlock/kitsch/ hack' movie against the respectability of literary criticism and academic film studies, making each term serve as a put-down but also an invitation to reclamation. In the *Oxford English Dictionary* schlock is defined as signifying 'cheap, shoddy or defective goods; inferior material, junk, "trash" (freq. applied to the arts or entertainment)'. The final note in Susan Sontag's 'Notes on Camp' is 'The ultimate Camp statement: it's good *because* it's awful…' (1983: 119). With roots in homosexual subcultures (derived from *se camper*; to flaunt), camp came to be adopted more generally as a mode of appreciation and appropriation that challenged dominant notions of taste. In the words of Andrew Ross, camp 'involves a celebration by the cognoscenti, of the alienation, distance, and incongruity reflected in the very processes of which hitherto unexpected value can be located in some obscure or exorbitant object' (1989: 146). The films he discusses, by directors such as John Waters, Russ Meyer and Hershell Gordon Lewis, tend to be the same as identified as trash cinema. In discussing Waters and *Trash* (the 1970 film directed by Paul Morrissey) Chuck Kleinhans refers to 'what I call trash – or deliberate low camp' (1993: 189).

Similarly, in a chapter on 'Camp Kitsch' in their volume *Kitsch!: Cultural Politics and Taste*, Ruth Holliday and Tracey Potts discuss Waters' 'camp aesthetic' as 'something of a terrorist assault on "good" taste', noting that 'Waters has become synonymous with the tacky and the trashy' (2012: 134). The German word *kitsch*, they note, is partly derived from 'kitschen', to collect junk from the street (2012: 47). Greenberg's dismissal of Hollywood movies in general as kitsch was another way of saying that they were junk or trash.

Words change their meaning. The desire of critics such as Greenberg and MacDonald to maintain lines of demarcation can be contrasted with the adoption of trash as a more fluid category. For Ernest Mathijs, trash cinema has become important for the challenge it provides to reception studies in the ways the films' reputation never seem to settle, moving in and out of favour. His example was the Harry Kümel-directed *Daughters of Darkness* (1971), a film 'described as both a masterwork *and* rubbish', and thus 'an excellent example for the study of the reception of trash cinema' (2005: 453). His conclusion was that the unfinished nature of the film's reception paralleled a significant shift in film studies. Since its release

> 'trash' has become a very different word in cinema studies. If it first referred to straightforward rubbish, it now carries a much more subtle and complex status. When, in a recent discussion of Kümel's work in *Sight & Sound*, *Daughters of Darkness* is introduced as 'commercial trash' the word is used in a far less negative way. It has come to signify a particular kind of film, characterised by its openness to different interpretations, much more than just a bad film. The change parallels a change in film discourse, in which issues of aesthetic quality have become less absolute, more dominated by what Jeffrey Sconce has called paracinematic taste. (2005: 471)

However this subtlety and complexity should not be seen as a straight path from negativity to openness. In the *Sight & Sound* discussion to which Mathijs refers it is in fact Kümel who is quoted as saying, 'For me it was commercial trash, just a film I did to make another' (Thompson 2002: 18). While Kümel used trash in a dismissive manner, a more recent *Sight & Sound* edition reveals the word invoked in other ways; making the case against Paul Verhoeven's *Elle* (2017), Ginette Vincendeau praised the performance of Isabelle Huppert but wrote that 'in the end she lends cultural legitimacy to a trashy movie masquerading as "post-feminist" intervention' (2017: 33); interviewed about her film *The Love Witch* (2016), Anne Biller explained that comments about disagreeing with the majority

of her reviews were 'because they use the word sexploitation, or exploitation, or sleaze, or trash, or any word that's tawdry or debased on purpose
as [if I'm doing this as a] joke' (Morgan 2017: 42). The opening up of an
understanding of trash as a form of open (avant-garde?) text has not led
to the disappearance of older, more negative connotations. At the same
time, the adoption of a negative term for different purposes brings with it
ambivalent connotations.

Paracinema and Trash Cinema

Within film studies, the notion of 'paracinema' has come to be central to
the understanding of trash. In '"Trashing" the Academy', Sconce (1995)
identified a distinct cineliteracy evident in contemporary fanzines and
books devoted to trash, and compared this 'paracinema' with critical and
theoretical approaches that film studies had taken on board in examining
Hollywood and alternative practices. From James Monaco's discussion of
the French New Wave to David Bordwell's notion of parametric narration
and Kristin Thompson's analysis of how stylistic excess can defamiliarise
the viewing experience, accounts of film history have emphasised the
potential of stylistic experimentation and deviance from norms (1995:
384–7). Within film studies, both the counter-cinema of Jean-Luc Godard
and the anti-illusionist melodramas of Douglas Sirk have been invoked as
a challenge to the dominance of classical Hollywood (1995: 392). Sconce's
variation on this was to argue for the radical potential of material poverty
and technical ineptitude rather than artistic bravado:

> paracinema might be said to succeed where earlier more 'radi-
> cal' avant gardes have failed … presenting a cinema so histrionic,
> anachronistic and excessive that it compels even the most casual
> viewer to engage it ironically, producing a relatively detached tex-
> tual space in which to consider, if only superficially, the cultural,
> historical and aesthetic politics that shape cinematic representa-
> tion. (1995: 393)

Underlying this was a debate about taste. Sconce's article drew on Pierre
Bourdieu's work on the class construction of taste, and the relationship
between economic, social and cultural capital. In Bourdieu's account,

cultural capital is built up through economic and social capital. However this does not mean that they exist at the same level, nor does cultural capital consist simply of preferring Wagner to Mantovani (as I. Q. Hunter and Heidi Kaye put it in their introduction to *Trash Aesthetics: Popular Culture and its Audience*, 1997: 3). Bourdieu linked the cultural capital of artistic perception to interest not only in 'the works designated for such apprehension, i.e. legitimate works of art, but everything in the world, including cultural objects which are not yet consecrated – such as, at one time, primitive arts, or, nowadays, popular photography or kitsch – and natural objects' (1984: xxvi). Sconce's variant on this was to argue that 'the discourses characteristically employed by paracinematic culture in its valorization of "low-brow" artefacts indicate that this audience, like the film elite (academic, aesthetes, critics), is particularly rich with "cultural capital" and thus possess a level of textual/critical sophistication similar to the cineastes they construct as their nemesis' (1995: 375). His claim about the radical potential of paracinema went further than that, in going beyond academic criticism's explanation of the disruptive potential of style and excess through 'a refined code of aesthetics' that had to be 'decoded by an elite cinephile in a rarefied and exclusive circuit of textual exchange' (1995: 392). Replacing Godard and the avant-garde with Edward D. Wood Jr. and trash could provide a more fundamental challenge to the sort of cultural hierarchies set out by MacDonald.

In one of the responses to this, Mark Jancovich argued that 'what Sconce calls "paracinema" is a species of bourgeois aesthetics, not a challenge to it' (2002: 311). The ironic reading and celebration of trash cinema 'may provide a limited challenge to academic practice, but it also shares much in common with it' (2002: 312). An anti-illusionist aesthetic belongs to the high-brow rather than the low, whether it is a response to the inept or the avant-garde filmmaker. In addition, for Jancovich, while Sconce acknowledged the disputes between different fan cultures, he failed to consider their implication. Cult, and trash, movie audiences do not share a uniformly oppositional attitude towards legitimate culture. Drawing on Sarah Thornton's adoption of the notion of 'sub-cultural capital' to explain distinctions within subcultures, Jancovich pointed out that the celebration of Wood's films included not only conservative commentators such as the Medved brothers but also a more oppositional stance based on looking down on others lacking in sub-cultural capital. From this perspective, rather than challenging elite values the cult of trash cinema itself constructs its own elite.

This picks up on tensions within Sconce's article. He presents paracinema as akin to academic criticism as well as a challenge to it. To put it one way: he discusses trashing the academy and trash in the academy. The place of ironic reading and the celebration of trash cinema within academia, and the conflicting pressures on graduate students 'not always willing to give up the excesses of the drive-in for the discipline of Dreyer' (1995: 378), is central to his concerns. He defines paracinema as a particular way of reading trash, but also as a way of valorizing trash (two not necessarily identical things). His comments on how 'the cultural politics of "trash culture" are becoming ever more ambiguous as this "aesthetic" grows in influence' (1995: 372) are themselves ambiguous in using trash as a label for a paracinematic culture as well as the material to which it is devoted. His emphasis on the ironic reading of trash cinema (quite distinct from the ironic use of the word 'trash') leaves questions about the extent to which this exhausts the significance of those films. The broader adoption of a paracinematic approach leaves questions about what this includes and excludes.

Others have subsequently addressed that gap, and the extent to which distinctions between a 'cult' and 'mainstream' audience itself creates its own hierarchy. Matt Hills has argued 'that we need to consider how notions of trash film have worked to exclude certain types of filmic sleaze that have also been simultaneously excluded from, or devalued within, academic discussion' (2007: 218). For Joanne Hollows, books such as *Incredibly Strange Films* but also academic responses to this material were marked by a tendency to naturalise cult as masculine and the mainstream as feminine, a tendency accentuated by the preoccupation with the 'sleazy', the 'hardcore' and the 'trashy' (2003: 38). Further, while 'associated with a challenge to cultural hierarchies and with resistance, transgression and radicalism, [cult] serves also to reproduce cultural distinctions and cultural hierarchies along the lines of gender' (2003: 49). Building on this, Jacinda Read contrasts national contexts, arguing that by being transplanted to a British context, Sconce's account of 'the graduate student's appropriation of trash cinema in terms of the generational or class politics of the canon' has been transformed into a concern with 'the problem of being a white, male, middle-class intellectual' and a reassertion of a 'masculine (sub)culture and politics in the face of the perceived institutionalization of feminism and its subsequent colonization and feminization of the margins' (2003: 59, 61).

From a different perspective, David Church argued that 'Sconce's (over) emphasis on the "badness" of some exploitation films plays down more traditional viewing pleasures that uneasily coexist with the profound negativity of paracinematic reading strategies ... there are many fans for whom paracinematic irony may not be the preferred mode of exploitation film consumption. There are, after all, many exploitation films that are [at] least competently made within their respective budgetary constraints, and many are not just critically championed by fans as inverted "great work"' (2016: 14, 15). In addition to stressing the extent to which knowledgeable working-class audiences could enjoy exploitation films for more than ironic laughs, he questioned the extent to which 'legitimate' cultural capital was needed to enjoy the pleasures of paracinematic irony: 'After all, if paracinema's apparent "badness" is largely measured by its perceived deviance from dominant Hollywood filmmaking norms, then so-called "mass" audiences should already be intuitively familiar with the mainstream conventions from which exploitation films seem to depart by virtue of their apparent aesthetic/economic impoverishment' (2016: 44).

Exploitation cinema, and trash cinema, can have affect beyond the benefits of an ironic perspective on the cultural, historical and aesthetic politics that shape cinematic representation or the satisfaction brought by filmmaking competence. As I. Q. Hunter puts it, 'Trash is appreciated along the nerves and in the guts and groin rather than coolly at a safe remove' (2013: 16). Trash cinema is linked here to what Linda Williams (1991) identified as 'body genres', designed to generate a physical rather than intellectual response: melodrama, horror, low comedy, pornography. For Joan Hawkins, the operative criterion for video catalogues appealing to a trash aesthetic was 'affect: the ability of a film to thrill, frighten, gross out, arouse, or otherwise directly engage the spectator's body' and it was this emphasis on affect that characterised 'paracinema as a low cinematic culture' (1999: 16). As Hawkins emphasised, this was complicated by the ways high and low could exist in proximity. Thus the mail order lists she came across in horror fanzines catalogued Carl Dreyer's *Vampyr* (1932) alongside *Tower of the Screaming Virgins* (1971), Jean-Luc Godard's *Weekend* (1968) next to *Zontar, the Thing from Venus*, while consumers of both high and low culture distinguished themselves from the mainstream.

Hills puts this slightly differently, writing that what Hawkins identified 'demonstrates that paracinema can be and has been revalued as film art by placing it in direct cultural proximity to films already deemed aesthetically (and legitimately) valuable' (2007: 221). In this context, the *Friday the 13th* franchise marks out the limits to paracinematic trash, largely excluded by both legitimate and trash film culture, the former for its sleazy, artless and formulaic nature, the latter on the grounds that it belongs to the mainstream.

The vocabulary used here is potentially confusing. Hills moves from Sconce's understanding of paracinema as a 'reading protocol' to 'Sconce's foundational study of trash cinema' (2007: 220). Does trash cinema refer to a group of films or to the reinterpretation of those films? In this book I distinguish between trash cinema and paracinema's devotion to trash cinema. That is, accepting the point that the *Friday the 13th* franchise 'has found itself languishing outside the sanctuary of legitimate culture as well as outside the trash-as-art revaluations of paracinema' (Hills 2007: 232), I still see it as useful to include the franchise under the umbrella of trash cinema, along with other films excluded by legitimate culture but not adopted for cult celebration. This is not because of a desire to reappropriate trash as a derogatory term but because of the value of not seeing trash and the paracinematic devotion to trash as one and the same. Trash cinema has taken on a particular importance because of its cult appropriation; but this appropriation does not exhaust the meaning of trash, and in discussing the topic of trash cinema it is important not to limit the discussion to films that have acquired cult status and to take note of the ways in which audiences construct their own cinema through their devotion to particular films.

Of course, trash cinema cannot be used as an entirely neutral label. It carries negative connotations even if only to turn them upside down. At the very least it is a term like 'punk', an insult that came to denote a particular form of music but which retains at least some of the aggression inherent in its adoption. More than that, trash cinema speaks of the complexity of taste formation and how this shifted across the twentieth century and beyond.

I am here inevitably drawing on my own experience as well as the accounts of others. That involved being introduced at an early age to arthouse fare from Bergman's *Through a Glass Darkly* (1961) to Godard's *Weekend*, and then gravitating to lower pleasures (1940s noir, 1950s science fiction, 1960s Hammer horror...) but as part of a wider, more omnivorous consumption. In the late 1970s and 1980s I went often enough to the Scala in London, more regularly to double, sometimes triple bills at the Electric, as well as to other London cinemas ranging from the NFT, the Essential, the Hampstead Everyman, the ICA to the Victoria Biograph. My visits to the Scala were as likely to be to see Dreyer's *The Passion of Joan of Arc* (1928) as Michael Miller's *Street Girls* (1975). The 'Cheap Thrills' season I went to in July 1979 at the ICA was not subtitled 'Trash, Movies and the Art of Transgression' but 'American Lowbudget Filmmaking': influenced by the publication of Todd McCarthy and Charles Flynn's *Kings of the Bs* (1975), it highlighted low-budget, genre filmmakers such as Edgar Ulmer but also screened the films of John Waters, Monte Hellman, Stephanie Rothman and Roger Corman. Cheap cinema was characterised here as radical but not the same way as was soon to be claimed for the films of Edward D. Wood Jr. On a visit to New York in 1980, though staying at the YMCA on 47th Street I never got to visit any of the grindhouse cinemas Bill Landis was starting to write about in *Sleazoid Express*. Instead I made my way up to the Thalia to see an Ulmer double bill of *Strange Illusion* (1945) and *Her Sister's Secret* (1946) and made use of the fact that late-night American television gave me access to the sort of minor old movies Michael Weldon was starting (unknown to me) to write about in *Psychotronic*. Television was central to my film education, but initially largely in the British context of a limited number of terrestrial channels. I didn't translate this often indiscriminate viewing into the discipline of Dreyer, who I already saw as up there on a par with Joseph H. Lewis and Roger Corman. This was not quite my version of John Waters' guilty pleasure (sneaking off to art films while posing as a 'trash film enthusiast' [1986: 108]), since my tastes spanned the high, the relatively low and the middlebrow. Studying, teaching and researching film has always meant looking at the popular, if often perhaps in forms that have now been legitimised, such as Hollywood melodrama and early film serials.

Building on this, the approach adopted here is inclusive rather than exclusive, and aims to provide a historical perspective on trash cinema. This book is not only about the 'nasty trash' of the 1970s and after. Putting this into perspective, the chapter that immediately follows provides a longer view, examining the period before 1960. In the main it does this not through how the films have been appropriated by later cult viewers. Discussion includes Dwain Esper's *Maniac* (1934) and Edward D. Wood Jr. but the aim is to place these and other films within their historical context. Trash is addressed here as a term that was used to denigrate rather than celebrate, and related to attempts to construct distinction within the American film industry. I examine the B-film but as part of broader construction of the different levels within the American film industry, examining how these operated and the extent to which individual films could move across them.

My concern with American cinema is retained in the following chapter, though here the focus shifts to the avant-garde and the Underground in the 1960s and the emergence of a more clearly identified trash cinema in the 1970s, in particular with the films of John Waters. That is, I examine the cultivation of a deliberate trash style, in an avant-garde and 'midnight movie' context, and (briefly) the longer term legacy of this.

The next chapter considers the period from 1980, the zines that were explicitly devoted to trash cinema, and the broader cult of trash that emerged and has persisted. Here the discussion becomes more international, if in part examined through American publications such as *European Trash Cinema*. Looking at trash as a cult provides an opportunity to examine the different ways in which this has taken place, from paracinematic irony to more traditional viewing pleasures.

Addressing such a broad territory has limited the space devoted to the analysis of individual films. This book is less a collection of readings of individual films than a discussion of how films have been read. That applies also to the final chapter. However, considering different versions and variations of *Flash Gordon* allows for a concluding overview of the lower reaches of cinema, from 1936 to the 1990s, and from the United States to Turkey.

There is much that could have been covered here but isn't. There is a lot of trash around and a short book cannot do justice to this extensive field. This book is not an attempt to identify key works of trash cinema; it sets out to explore what trash means, and has meant, in the cinema, and the questions raised by this. The aim is to explore trash cinema, to test its limits, rather than to simply understand it as a fixed category.

2   BEFORE THE 1960s: FROM B TO Z

In 1930 *Motion Picture News* reported on a new trend among Chicago cinemagoers:

> Numerous neighbourhood houses here which draw a sophisticated or 'smart' audience, are booking a number of melodramas, western, serials and the like, with the result that independent product is getting its best play here in years...
>
> The meller stuff is clicking in every spot where the trade approaches the highbrow. Audiences give the mellers a big hand; the cheaper and more ludicrous the picture, the better it is liked. The trend, in consequence, though no doubt little more than a fad, is beginning to be looked upon here as genuine competition for legitimate short subject product, which it is replacing.
>
> Recognition of this trend in popular taste, though naturally in a more modified vein, is being given even by circuit bookings. Publix, Warner and Fox theatres here have booked independent product, largely serials and westerns. Originally the bookings were for kids' matinees and did not show at evening performances. Adults, however, 'went' for the cheap product in such numbers and with so much enthusiasm that it became a problem for a kid to get a seat at one of the matinees. (Anon. 1930)

A similar 'smart' interest in 'trashy' genres (but not limited to a temporary fad) had been noted at New York's Rialto cinema in the 1930s and 1940s, leading Tim Snelson and Mark Jancovich to identify that cinema as 'a critical venue for the emergence of the cult movie scene, a phenomenon that is usually associated with the 1950s, 1960s or 1970s' (2011: 200–1).

As Steve Chibnall notes, it was the early 1980s that saw 'a wave of American publications dedicated to "bad" and "cult" films' (1997: 85). That dedication included earlier films, though not usually those made earlier than the 1950s. Trash has often been associated with the 1950s and after, in publications from *Trash: The Graphic Genius of Xploitation Movie Posters* (Boyreau 2002) (described on the cover as an assembly of 'more than 150 masterpieces of twisted brilliance, lowbrow graphic poster art from the sickest, sleaziest, sexiest, and weirdest films from the 1950s through the 1980s') to I. Q. Hunter's observation that, 'The roll call of essential British trash begins with David MacDonald's *Devil Girl from Mars* (1954)' (2015: 32). Where the B-film is linked to trash cinema it has been traced back as far as the 1950s but rarely further. Thus Jack Stevenson's 'confessions of a B-movie archaeologist' includes a 'secret history of cult movies' that begins in 1953 and a section on 'Camp and Trash' in which he identifies the trash movie aesthetic as 'founded on an appreciation for the low-budget commercial B-films of the fifties and sixties' (2003: 47, 126). In many ways the key work on the American B-film is still Charles Flynn and Todd McCarthy's anthology, *Kings of the Bs: Working within the Hollywood System* (1975a). However, while this includes a historical account of the emergence of the B-film in the 1930s and interviews with filmmakers working in that decade, the earliest film discussed at any length is *The Stranger on the Third Floor* (1940). Contributions to the anthology tend to focus on the 1940s, 1950s or 1960s.

There is solid justification for locating a growing cult interest in cinema within the later decades of the twentieth century, and in going on to explore the 'cult of trash' my own account will focus on publications from the 1980s and after. With the significant exception of the 1930s exploitation films directed or distributed by Dwain Esper, in general publications celebrating the trash qualities of cinema have not focused on the first half of the twentieth century. Trash can be invoked in discussions of films from that earlier period, but in a different way. In 'Of Trash and Treasure', William Cline argued that people who dismissed serials and B-westerns as trash made unfair comparisons with films such as *Gone with the Wind* (1939), *Casablanca* (1942) and *The Best Years of Our Lives* (1946) (1994: 6). In contrast to Lester Bang's 'fuck those people who'd rather be watching *The Best Years of Our Lives* or *David and Lisa* [1962]. We got our own good tastes...' (quoted in Sconce 1995: 371), Cline's more modest and conservative purpose was to argue that the films he wrote about should not be compared with the classics of Hollywood, as they were 'produced for the sole purpose of providing immediate, familiar, but unpretentious entertainment for people who like their films simple and straightforward' and on that basis 'a good western or a good serial is a "treasure" rather than "trash"' (1994: 6).

Trade press reports such as the one quoted above, as well as research such as that done on New York's Rialto, point to a longer-standing highbrow interest in the low. Aside from this cult interest, in an examination of trash cinema and of construction of how distinctions operated within the American film industry it is useful to look at least as far back as the 1930s, the decade when the B-film emerged as a recognised part of the process of production, distribution and exhibition. According to Ben Taves, 'roughly 75 percent of the pictures made during the 1930s, well over four thousand films, fall under the B rubric' (1995: 313). While this figure does not distinguish between the B-films of the major studios and the products of the independent, 'Poverty Row' studios, it highlights a mass of films excluded from most film histories of the period. The very notion of a B-film also indicates the construction of the cultural hierarchies central to the designation of areas of cinema as trash. Thus in this chapter I focus first on the 1930s, then on the 1940s and 1950s. This overview will include the films of Dwain Esper and Edward D. Wood Jr. but rather than just examine these in terms of their cult celebration, the purpose here is to place them within their historical context, looking more generally at the B-film, Poverty Row and the different forms of exploitation cinema, as well as at the 'Main Street' theatre, the grindhouse and the drive-in. This also means looking at how trash has been understood not just as a form of cult cinema but also as a negative term of rejection and derogation.

The 1930s

Two quotes from 1934 illustrate the different forms taken by the condemnation of Hollywood as trash. 'Of her many American pictures, all without exception have been trash', wrote Paul Rotha of Greta Garbo's performance in MGM's *Queen Christina* (1932), 'yet this astonishing woman surmounts the very crudity with which they choose to surround her' (1934: 185). The same year *Parent's Magazine* warned that all their fine efforts to select films suitable for children 'may be offset if a picture is presented on a program along with cheap and trashy pictures' (quoted in Jacobs 1992: 1). Trash could be associated with Hollywood in general, and with the prestige MGM picture as well as with the low-budget production, or it could be identified with the bottom half of the double bill, or below. It could also be used either to elevate a film star or film, in the discovery of treasure among the trash, or to derogate a film or a body of films.

The context of this was in part the efforts of critics to select and distinguish. It was also a consequence of the efforts of those within the film industry who were concerned to promote Hollywood's 'better pictures', designed to appeal to higher earners and appease moral campaigners (see Maltby 1995: 62). The concern had been longstanding but it took on particular significance with the establishment of the Production Code as a means of regulating what films were made and shown, and a broader policy of promoting literary adaptations and historical biographies rather than less elevating material. The growth of the double bill was also a key factor.

The double bill, a show which combined two feature-length films, had been part of the cinema-going experience for some while, but the practice became more prevalent in the 1930s, when Depression-era cinemas were resorting to whatever means they had at their disposal to encourage regular attendance. In order to keep costs down and the programme viable, the second part of the double bill tended to be a shorter and less expensive film. In the early 1930s this part of the programme was often supplied by one of the smaller studios located in the suburb of Los Angeles that had become known as Gower Gulch or Poverty Row. Concern that this would diminish their share of the exhibition market led the Hollywood majors to set up B-production units, making films that were shorter than their A-pictures, and had lesser-known stars, lower budgets and shorter schedules. In a number of instances, B-films existed as part of a series, for instance the Mr Moto films made at 20th Century-Fox, starting with *Think Fast Mr Moto* (1937), an approach that could keep down cost but also compensate for the relative lack of recognition caused by the absence of a major star. These more cheaply produced films were not promoted to the extent of an A-film and were also separated through the distribution process, with independent exhibitors renting unidentified blocks of films differentiated by whether they were paid for through a percentage of the box-office take (in the case of the A-film) or through a flat fee (the B).

For those worrying about 'trashy pictures' the double bill was a potential threat. Complaints such as those expressed in *Parent's Magazine* were echoed elsewhere. Contributors to *Film Daily*, for instance, were alarmed about 'the many truly fine photoplays which have been smeared with the trash of a second feature' (17 May 1937) and wrote on topics such as 'Duals, Trash and Trailers' (18 May 1937). However the B-film could exist as a response to the economic and moral threat of Poverty Row. In this sense the 1930s B-film did not so much occupy the disreputable end of Hollywood production as a slightly lower rung on the ladder. One of the earliest examples I have seen of a specific film being identified as a B-film is a *Motion Picture Herald* review of 13 March 1937 which described *The Outcasts of Poker Flat* (1937) as 'A better than average B'. Directed by Christy Cabanne for RKO, it was one of a number of films based on Bret Harte's 1869 story of the same name, and followed on from John Ford's version of 1919. It has similarities to other Ford films, particularly *Stagecoach* (1939) and *My Darling Clementine* (1946), in its narrative of childbirth, gambling, drunken Native Americans and ambivalence towards the Wild West making way for a world of schools and churches. Where it differs from the Ford films is in the absence of the quickening of pace found in the stagecoach attacks in *Stagecoach* and the myth-inspiring possibilities of the landscape of the West characteristic of Ford's work more generally. Like many other B-films, *The Outcasts of Poker Flat* remains dialogue-based and largely interior while keeping firmly within the codes and conventions of classical Hollywood.

The studio B-film belonged to the Hollywood hierarchy of the Big Five producers, distributors and exhibitors (MGM, Paramount, 20th Century-Fox, Warners and RKO) and Little Three producers/distributors (Universal, Columbia and United Artists). At the low end of that group, Universal produced a small number of prestige pictures, but specialised in low-budget features, shorts and serials, operating in a territory closer to Poverty Row than MGM. At the high end of Poverty Row, Republic Pictures aspired to compete with the majors but also distinguished between their own films. Their Jubilee pictures were mainly westerns, with seven-day shooting schedules and $50,000 budgets, Anniversary pictures had fourteen- to fifteen-day shooting schedules and budgets of between $175,000 and $200,000, in contrast to higher budgeted Delux and Premiere films (see Flynn and McCarthy 1975b: 25–30). Lower down on Poverty Row were companies such as Peerless, Puritan, Reliable and various companies operated by Max, Louis and Adolph Weiss. Quickly made in rented lots, they were distributed through the States Rights system, which involved flat-fee sales to specific territories for limited periods.

Thus, as Yannis Tzioumakis notes, 'the labels B and Poverty Row are not synonymous' (2006: 73). Indeed, Poverty Row can be understood as involved in a fundamentally different form of film production and film style, and appealing to different audience expectations and often different audiences. With no pretensions to MGM quality, their films were directed at audiences with little interest in classically structured narratives and instead tended to emphasise relentless action, often to the detriment of coherence, mood and characterisation (2006: 76). They may have been trash by the standards of the Hollywood majors and *Parent's Magazine* columnists but they provided those who were watching them something that 'better pictures' did not.

Some qualification is needed here. Major studio Universal produced Buck Jones western serials that were as action-based as any film being made at the time, while a Poverty Row title such as *Murder at Glen Athol*, directed by Frank Strayer for Invincible, is an adaptation of a 'Crime Club' novel that is a dialogue-based mystery story with minimal action and a cast often in evening dress. It was one of eight 1936 films under the Invincible banner released by Chesterfield, a company identified by Michael Pitts as the longest running of the Poverty Row studios (1997: 83). Chesterfield, Pitts notes, eschewed 'westerns and outdoor actioners for indoor dramas and comedies shot on rented studio space' (1997: 85).

Victor Adamson Productions can stand in for a company at the lower end of Poverty Row, and *Rawhide Terror* (1934) for a western from the lower reaches of Poverty Row. When Robert S. Birchard compiled a list of filmmakers whose work was every bit as demented as that of the notorious Edward D. Wood Jr., Victor Adamson, also known as Denver Dixon, was the first on his list: 'In Dixon's cinema every cut was a mismatch, every

Fig. 1: Class values
in Poverty Row's
Murder at Glen Athol

actor an amateur, and every plot incomprehensible' (1995: 451). This is a
little unfair to someone like William Desmond, one of a number of silent
film stars who ended up appearing in serials and short features such as
Rawhide Terror. The film undeniably has its narrative confusions. Written
and supervised by Adamson/Dixon (father of Al Adamson, who went on
to employ his father on films such as *Satan's Sadists* [1969]), but directed
by Bruce Mitchell and Jack Nelson, *Rawhide Terror* was reputedly intended
as a serial but turned into a short feature when it became apparent that
was as far as the funds would stretch. This may explain the narrative gaps.
A subplot about an abusive stepfather disappears half way, while Jimmy,
the stepson, becomes Tommy and then Jimmy again. It is not the only
name change. Abrupt jumps in time make the story, and the identity of
individual characters, difficult to follow, though the film remains an interesting generic hybrid, mixing the western and horror film.

   It is not as demented as Dwain Esper's *Maniac* (1934), which Tim Lucas
described as 'perhaps the earliest film to assemble all the essentials
of trash' (2015: 27), and which Jeffrey Sconce categorised as 'sub-zero
degree cinema' (2003: 18). Pitts includes Esper's Road Show Attractions
in his list of Poverty Row companies (1997: 324–9), but Esper is more
commonly identified as an exploitation filmmaker. What Eric Schaefer
(1999) refers to as the 'classical exploitation film' existed in parallel with
classical Hollywood cinema between the end of the First World War and
the end of the 1950s but was distinguished from it through its minimal

budgets and production values and in its commitment to forbidden spectacle (scenes of nudity, childbirth, drug taking, etc. that would not have been permitted in a major studio production) rather than narrative coherence. *Maniac* reputedly cost around $7,500 (see Schaefer 1999: 51). It follows the standard exploitation conceit of purporting to deliver a moral lesson (the 'square-up'), beginning with a scrolling text foreword in which 'Wm. S. Sadler, M.D., F.A.C.S, Director of the Chicago Institute of Research' cautions of 'the disastrous results of fear thought [sic] not only on the individual but on the nation' and which ends with the warning that 'Unhealthy thought creates warped attitudes which in turn create criminals and manias'. Similar titles periodically reappear, as when the shooting of mad scientist Dr Mierschultz by his vaudeville impersonator/criminal-on-the-run assistant Don Maxwell is followed by an explanatory title beginning, 'Dementia praecox patients show blunting of the emotions, serious defects of judgment, development of fantastic ideas, belief that they are being forced to do things or are being interfered with.' Elements of the stories of Edgar Allan Poe are mixed with the forbidden spectacle of scantily-dressed women, though the film is most notorious for the scene in which Don, now impersonating Mierschultz, captures a cat that has eaten a human heart revived by the mad scientist, gouges out one of the cat's eyes and eats the eyeball, laughing maniacally and declaring, 'Why, not unlike an oyster or a grape.' Eyeball-eating was not something shown in the major studio productions.

Maniac is characterised by the need for the classic exploitation film to show what other films could not under the veneer of a moral and scientific message and/or using entertainment as justification. The film ends with Don, now behind bars, declaring: 'I only wanted to amuse, to entertain.' It is also marked by histrionic performances and a failure to produce (or disinterest in producing) anything close to continuity filmmaking. The relationship between shots is often unclear, characters appear and disappear with little explanation, and the black cat chased by Don becomes a much lighter tabby when in the hands of the impersonator. For Schaefer this demonstrates how spectacle was more important than story in the exploitation film (1999: 93), for Sconce the 'grammatical irrationality' of the film has an ironic pedagogic consequence, having the potential to allow students to use filmmaking 'failure' to understand film language more generally (2003: 30). For Robert Weiner, the film is less a faulty narrative than a counter-narrative, in which the incoherence is part of the point, making the film akin to the avant-garde in its significance if not its intent (2010: 49). Notwithstanding those smart Chicago audiences mentioned at the beginning of this chapter, Weiner's point seems more relevant to recent interest in Esper than to the 1930s, but each of these explanations is based on a justifiable understanding of the film as operating in a different territory to others of the time. At the same time, even in the 1930s there was movement across different strands of cinema.

The Lost City (1935) is a case in point. This twelve-chapter serial was directed by Harry Revier for Shermann Krellberg's Super-Serial Productions. As a form of cinema, the serial (episodic narratives of between ten and fifteen chapters, which individually tended to last around twenty minutes) had been marginalised by the 1930s to the children's matinee, the neighbourhood cinema and the overseas market. However, what these lacked in prestige they made up for in numbers, and in the second half of the 1930s the serial even achieved a degree of prominence with, for instance, Universal's *Flash Gordon* films. *The Lost City* was at the lower end of this market. It was quickly and cheaply filmed by a director whose career had included major box-office successes (in 1920 he directed a pair of *Tarzan* films) but whose next assignment was the exploitation film, *Lash of the Penitentes* (1936), a combination of documentary footage of the secretive Los Hermanos Penitentes sect and a drama about a writer investigating the sect, spiced with scenes of female nudity. Krellberg, the producer of *The Lost City*, operated also as a financier, distributor and exhibitor, with an interest in 'legitimate' theatre as well as cinemas, and bringing films such as Carl Dreyer's *The Passion of Joan of Arc* to America, if in doctored form. In order to draw the maximum revenue from his minimal production output, Krellberg released *The Lost City* as both a serial *and* a feature. He released a further feature version in 1943, renamed *The City of Lost Men*, under which title it played on a double-bill with Fritz Lang's 1931 film *M* (now called *M – The Kidnapper*), to the bewilderment of reviewers. In its different forms this crude jungle melodrama with science fiction trimmings moved from children's matinees to action houses, and screenings across Latin America and Asia to the arthouse (see Barefoot 2017: 84–9).

Distinctions here thus operated not just in a film's production base but through distribution and exhibition. The definition of the B-film as forming the lower part of a double-bill highlights the significance of exhibition

Fig. 2: Advertisement
for screening of *City
of Lost Men* (*The
Lost City*) with *M* at
the Strand Cinema,
Cincinnati

practices, but as well as operating within the programme, film industry
hierarchy existed through distinctions between cinemas. Cinemas were
classified as first-run, second-run, third-run and so on, with distinctions
operating in terms of location and pricing as well as the age and type of
film. A film released by one of the majors had a fluid status based on the
reception it received (a 'sleeper' made as a B-film might be upgraded to
A-status while a less popular A-film could go in the other direction) as well
as its age, as a film released in first-run cinemas over time moved down
the chain and perhaps up and down the programme. Poverty Row films,
however, rarely reached the first-run cinemas and while some neighbourhood cinemas showed major A-films a while after their initial release,
others specialised in westerns, serials and other action-based films produced by Columbia, Universal or Poverty Row. This was particularly the
case with the grindhouse cinemas, named after the policy of continuous
screenings at varying prices. In retrospect, it is tempting to view these
subsequent-run screenings as being on the margins. However, as Phyll
Smith demonstrates, grindhouse screenings in the 1930s (and other decades) were less a minority practice than 'the bedrock of the Hollywood
industry' (2016: 47), never making any great profit but significant because

of the number of people who saw films at the grindhouse rather than the first-run house.

Exploitation films were anyway excluded from those cinemas affiliated to the industry trade organisation, the Motion Picture Producers' Association, who would only show films with the MPAA's Production Code of approval. They were screened in the relatively small number of 'Main Street' cinemas that specialised in their field, on an irregular basis by the much larger number of independent cinemas which showed a mix of films from the majors and Poverty Row but were not averse to generating additional box-office returns though more sensationalist material, or through road-showing (travelling from location to location with the film) or 'four-walling' (leasing the premises rather than taking a cut of the box-office). They could have a remarkably long life: Schaefer notes that Revier peddled *Lash of the Penitentes* (made for around $15,000) under the title *The Penitentes Murder Case* for a year before selling it to Mike J. Levinson, who kept it in circulation for decades (1999: 64). This is one of the ironies of trash cinema: it can often have a much longer life than films accorded more respect.

From the 1940s to the 1960s

In a review contrasting a series of French low-budget TV features about teenagers with a set of related but different American 'Drive-In Classics' that reimagined AIP films from the 1950s, Jonathan Rosenbaum dismissed the idea that the latter were based on B-films. In his account, in the 1950s teenagers with enough pocket money and autonomy led to a completely new strain of filmmaking and film-going: 'For virtually the first time, "bad" movies that teenagers could feel superior or at least equal to became a significant part of movie culture' (2016). For Rosenbaum, this was not the naïve 'badness' evident in the films of Edward D. Wood Jr., but the 'more calculated and ironic "badness" of a Corman quickie', though 'only later generations, with their approximate grasp of film history and market distinctions, would call both of them B-movies' (ibid.).

Did, then, the 1950s see the B-movie change into the Bad movie, albeit one that came with different varieties of badness? This would be in line with the tendency (noted at the beginning of this chapter) to date trash cinema from the 1950s. In fact, it is tempting to adapt Rosenbaum's

Fig. 3: *I Walked with a Zombie* and the visual poetry of the B-film

argument by positing different trends in the 1940s and 1950s, in the earlier decade towards the 'quality B-movie', in the latter towards the 'bad B-movie'.

The 'quality B-movie' of the 1940s can explain the tendency for B-movie overviews to cite films from that decade rather than earlier. Films such as *I Walked with a Zombie* (1943), *When Strangers Marry* (1944) and *Detour* (1945) demonstrate that B-unit or Poverty Row origins did not preclude high filmmaking standards. Thus, *I Walked with a Zombie* has been praised as a major achievement from its director, Jacques Tourneur, and producer, Val Lewton, notwithstanding its origins as an RKO B-unit film with a pulp fiction title. This is evident through the visual poetry of scenes such as the night-time walk to the Homefort, a sequence of almost four minutes without dialogue, as well as an overall audio-visual style based on shadow and suggestion that allowed Carlos Clarens to identify it as standing out 'as chamber music against the seedy bombast of the claw-and-fang epics of the day' (quoted in Jancovich 2012: 21), and a remarkable thematic complexity in its concern with ethnicity, science and superstition, and dysfunctional family life.

The Poverty Row film noir has also lent itself to a variation on this approach. In 'Beatitudes of B Pictures', Andrew Sarris distinguished between the trivia hound who 'loves all B pictures simply because they are B pictures' and the treasure hunter who 'loves only certain B pictures because they have somehow overcome the onus of having started out as B pictures' (1975: 49). As a treasure hunter with a hint of the trivia hound he praised Monogram's *When Strangers Marry* as 'a not bad William Castle imitation of Alfred Hitchcock in which the three leads give the film an A gloss' (1975: 52). Also praising the film, and more generally 'the unspectacular B, worked out by a few people with belief and skill in their art, who capture the unworked over immediacy of life before it has been cooled by "art"', Manny Farber, wrote of Castle's experimentation with the 'then new Hollywood idea of shooting without studio lights in the sort of off-Broadway rented room where time seems to stand still for years and the only city sounds come through a postage-stamp opening on the air well' (1975: 45). The notion of Poverty Row as enabling experimentation but also lending authenticity to the film is probably most closely connected to PRC's *Detour*. The visual style of the film can be explained by the freedom given to director Edgar Ulmer on account of his de facto Head of Production status at the studio but also through how the studio's limited resources help to give the film the sordid look of Poverty Row. The noir clichés of the dialogue accentuates the pulp nature of the material, as when a ten-buck tip provokes central character Al Roberts to say, in his interior monologue, 'What was it, I asked: a piece of paper crawling with germs.' The result was a film to be valued not for overcoming its seedy origins but for providing a closer look at those origins.

The industrial context to this was the move towards the B-film as an increasingly uncertain category. In Paul Kerr's words, one result was the B film noir, 'an ambitious B, a B bidding for critical and/or commercial prestige' (1983: 52). However, here the term becomes stretched. Praising Joseph H. Lewis's *Gun Crazy* (1949), Jim Kitses defined it as 'B-movie poetry, B-movie tragedy, B-movie movie' (1996: 70). He also noted that that the film had an estimated $400,000 budget, contrasting with the budgets of around $16,000 given to Lewis when he worked for Poverty Row studio Monogram in the early 1940s (1996: 80 n5), making films that have received much less critical attention. 'B' is adopted as a value, in line with Farber's notion of capturing the unworked over immediacy of life, evident in Lewis's use of bravura camerawork and the intensity of the performances of John Dall and Peggy Cummins in *Gun Crazy*.

This sort of 'B-movie poetry' can be traced in the 1950s but in a world in which the studio system B-film has even less of an existence and in which the William Castle who experimented with light and sound in *When*

Strangers Marry made way for William Castle the showman director-producer of *Macabre* (1958), promoted with a $1,000 insurance policy (see
Anon. 1958). As Blair Davis (2012) has pointed out, the B-film remained
part of industry discourse, with major studios producing modestly budg-
eted films alongside blockbusters and the emergence of new companies
specialising in the low-budget market. What was disappearing was the old
B-film. By the 1950s the major studio B-units had been closed down and
the block booking system had ended, meaning that exhibitors bought films
individually rather than as part of package. For some time the majors had
been placing increasing emphasis on a smaller number of more expensive films. Declining and less regular audiences, cinema closures and the
growth of television threatened low-budget films produced by major and
minor studios alike. The big-screen western in particular, which had played
a central part in the studio B-film and Poverty Row production, now had to
compete with a proliferation of small screen versions. Western specialist
Republic ended up selling its films to television and ceased film production in 1958. By the end of the decade the exploitation film was facing its
own challenges, from Hollywood films such as *The Man with the Golden
Arm* (1955) which dealt with drugs or other formerly forbidden topics, and
racier European imports such as *...And God Created Woman* (1956).

The 1950s was also a decade that saw an overall decline in cinema
attendance, moderated only by the event movie at the high end of the
market and the rise of the drive-in at the low end. The first drive-in had
been established in 1933 but this form of exhibition only took off in the
1950s. Its expansion was significant: in 1953 drive-in cinemas accounted
for over 20 per cent of the total box-office (see Davis 2012: 36). The drive-
in has come to be linked to the teenager, whether through a relatively
innocent, 1950s image in which young Americans, with more money than
earlier generations of teenagers and a greater access to the car, using the
drive-in as a dating ground, or a latter version of the drive-in as the site of
exploitation movies, the 'Blood, Breasts, and Beasts' movies celebrated
in publications such as *Joe Bob Briggs Goes to the Drive-In* (see Briggs
1989: 10). In this sense, 'drive-in' has come to change its meaning just
as 'grindhouse' has, both now associated with a trashy form of American
exploitation cinema. Initially, however, the main appeal of the drive-in
was to the family, though also to different audiences that tended to avoid
traditional ('hard-top') cinemas, including teenagers but also working-

class, obese, non-white, female or disabled audiences. In the 1960s the playgrounds that had been set up in drive-ins were taken down (see Segrave 1992: 189) and over time less emphasis was placed on the family audience, though drive-ins continued to screen a range of films even into the 1970s, including mainstream new releases as well as out-and-out exploitation, and to appeal to different audiences, with significant seasonal variations.

Teenagers did make up one part of the drive-in audience and one that became increasingly significant for the film industry in the 1950s, and to the independents in particular. The Hollywood majors had traditionally presented themselves as appealing to a universal audience, with a system of regulation designed so that films were acceptable to everyone. They were slow to respond to trade press reports that, as *Variety* put in 1956, the 1950s were 'Hollywood's Age of the Teens' (quoted in Davis 2012: 39). Independent companies such as American International Pictures (AIP) were quicker, deliberately pitching their films at a youth market, and developing a new form of exploitation film. These were not the earlier 'adults only' exploitation films which could abandon narrative logic or narrative as a whole in their concern with forbidden spectacle. However, they shared an emphasis on showmanship with earlier forms of exploitation, promoting their films with sensationalist titles and advertisements, raising expectations that the films themselves struggled to fulfil.

Roger Corman played a central role in this, if also an ambiguous one. Corman was a key figure at AIP in the 1950s though his work rate was so high that he also made films for other companies. In 1957 alone he completed *Attack of the Crab Monsters, Carnival Rock, Naked Paradise, Not of This Earth, Rock All Night, The Saga of the Viking Women and their Voyage to the Waters of the Great Sea Serpent, She Gods of Shark Reef, Sorority Girl, Teenage Doll, The Undead* and *War of the Satellites*. He kept costs low through rapid production turnaround and low wages. During the filming process the emphasis was primarily placed on setting up as many shots as possible during the day. Costs could be further reduced by shooting films back-to-back, recycling sets and using actors in multiples roles. The emphasis was on speed and efficiency of production: 'It was pretty much "Do it quick"' according to actor Mike Connors. 'There wasn't a lot of acting direction going on. For him it was where to set up the camera and how to make the most of the time he had' (quoted in Davis 2012: 117).

For Jeffrey Sconce, the limited resources given to Corman, as well as other director-producers such as David F. Friedman, William Castle and Hershell Gordon Lewis, was a key factor in their paracinematic following. They have become

> folk heroes in this community by acknowledging, even embracing, the fundamental hucksterism of all cinema, each in his own way a cynical pragmatist unencumbered by the delusions of art and gravitas that afflict more deluded filmmakers. ... Corman stands as patron saint of a bygone era when a filmmaker – despite irritable cameras, questionable film stock, bad sound takes, lousy actors, flubbed lines or botched continuity – could still take on twenty-five set-ups a day and finish a film in a week. ... For many trash cinephiles, this is the essence of the art form, a medium of exploitation that has always been less about realizing some idealized artistic vision than the act of creation itself, transforming the cinema as a whole into an existential metaphor of affirmation in the face of chaotic absurdity. (2007b: 288)

What this doesn't fully explain is the particular attention paid to Corman rather than numerous other filmmakers working with impoverished resources but still managing to come up with as many or even more set-ups in a day. In the 1930s and 1940s for instance, serial directors such as William Witney, and even less well-known filmmakers such as Ray Taylor, had a remarkable rate of production on minimal budgets. They differ partly because they worked within much more regimented formulae. Corman worked with genre material but across a range of genres. His 1957 work alone combined science fiction with the teen film, South Sea adventures, the crime film, the Viking saga, a college-set melodrama and a film about a woman whose regression through past lives takes her back to the Middle Ages. A film such as *Not of This Earth* recycles horror and science fiction conventions in its narrative of threat from aliens who need regular blood infusion, but also varies them through outfitting the vampire with a suit and dark glasses and looks to slightly later work such as *A Bucket of Blood* (1959) and *The Little Shop of Horrors* (1960) in its use of comedy. In a different way, *Sorority Girl* achieves a peculiar intensity by playing up the melodrama and sadomasochism of its story of collegiate and family

Fig. 4: The vampire
in modern dress,
between police
and nurse, in
Not of This Earth

power relations. Here and elsewhere Corman's films of the 1950s retained an appeal both through their papier-mâché and chicken-wire monsters but also because they contain additional distinctive qualities in their imagery, performance or ideas.

Corman's efficient cynicism at least contrasts with that of another director-producer who started making films in the 1950s: Jerry Warren. Blair Davis cites Warren as an example of the apathetic director, quoting his reply to the suggestion that they do something *good* for a change; 'Why? People aren't interested in anything good, they don't know and they don't care. Just give them garbage!' (2012: 192). The result in 1956 was *Man Beast*, an Abominable Snowman variation possibly made for less than $30,000, using stock footage for its action scenes, a series of different actors in a Yeti suits, shots framed against a black background to avoid the cost of dressing a set, and a succession of continuity errors. This was, in Warren's own account, filmmaking designed to be good enough to be bought by a distributor but no better. If nothing else, Warren's films and his approach to filmmaking can help counter romantic notions of the low-budget auteur. They demonstrate how low-cost cinema often failed to adhere to the standards of classical Hollywood. While the errors in *Man Beast* are less striking than those found elsewhere, this pushes the film towards dullness rather than the sublimely or even naively bad.

The work of Corman and Warren help put the films of Edward D. Wood Jr. into some kind of perspective. The 'elevation' of Wood to the status

of 'worst director of all time', and subsequently to the romantic figure of
Tim Burton's *Ed Wood* (1994), has tended to separate him from his time.
Wood's *Plan 9 from Outer Space* (1959) was one of numerous science fiction films of the period. *Motion Picture Herald* reviewed it as 'but another
in the apparently endless stream of minor-effort sci-fi, played out with
an obvious eye on the type of audience that is not particularly concerned
with logic and clamors only for weirdness, the further out in the unknown
areas the better' (quoted in Davis 2012: 191). Similarly, Wood's *Bride of
the Monster* (1955) was, for *Motion Picture Daily*, another in 'the unending
stream of horror melodramas', following 'in a familiar vein' (Anon. 1956).
Motion Picture Herald even mildly praised that film, suggesting that Bela
Lugosi and other cast members 'go through the assigned action and
dialogue of the Wood-Alex Gordon screenplay with something approaching briskness and the film benefits accordingly' (quoted in Davis 2012:
191). In the context of the 1950s, what is most notable about Wood is
the extent to which he was a marginal figure. His films received a minimal initial release and appear to have been seen by a limited number of
people in the decade. This was particularly the case with *Glen or Glenda*
(1953). 'I had a tough time selling this one', said producer George Weiss.
'Because the burlesque type of house wouldn't want it because it was
too highbrow. ... The picture didn't actually make any money. I couldn't
even sell England. It was ahead of it's [sic] time' (quoted in Grey 1995:
43). Wood's significance thus rests largely in how later cult and camp
audiences adopted him and his films. However, *Glen or Glenda*, his first
feature-length film, does stand out as a remarkable film, for its failings,
content and the treatment of that content.

Glen or Glenda belongs to the older tradition of exploitation film. George Weiss's career in exploitation films began with *Test Tube Babies* (1948), while cinematographer William C. Thompson, who also photographed *Plan 9 From Outer Space*, had earlier worked on Esper's *Maniac*. Originally intended as a documentary about Christine Jorgensen's sex change (from George Jorgensen), it became a more curious film with the hiring of Wood's friend Bela Lugosi to play 'The Scientist', commenting on events in the film. The result is a mix of different films and film styles. It is in part an old-fashioned exploitation film, complete with opening titles ending 'You are Society ... Judge Ye Not!' and sex-change operation scenes for forbidden spectacle. Alongside this is a transvestite drama, given an autobiographical edge by being acted out with Wood himself playing Glen, the transvestite in the film, and his real-life partner Dolores Fuller playing Glen's partner, Barbara. The footage of Lugosi surrounded by skulls, skeletons and other Gothic trappings form a third side to the film. In addition, Weiss later reported that he added additional footage because he needed to push the running length up to 70 minutes (see Grey 1995: 46).

Wood's own transvestism, and the presence of a number of other transvestites in the film, turned *Glen or Glenda* into a documentary of sorts. Thus, though subsequent interest has been in the film's failings it has also fascinated as a glimpse into another side of 1950s America, and for its sympathetic treatment of transvestism and transsexuality, alongside an insistence on the normality of these people and a resistance to any suggestion of homosexuality. As Sconce put it, 'Set against the bland cultural miasma of the Eisenhower years, Wood and his film stand out as truly remarkable figures' (1995: 389), though they perhaps point to complications within that miasma. There seems to be little information on its contemporary reception. In contrast, it has gone on to attract significant attention, whether as a 'bad film', an avant-garde film, or at least working like one in drawing attention to the cinematic apparatus. It is notable both for the earnest quality of its performances and for its bizarre use of stock footage – the latter being not unusual for low-budget filmmaking, but here for the manner in which it is used, far beyond apparent necessity, often in a seemingly arbitrary way. The shot of stampeding buffalo that interrupts a conversation between the transvestite Glen and his partner Barbara is but one, albeit particularly striking, example.

Fig. 6: In *Glen or Glenda*, Glen comes close to confessing his angora fetish...

Fig. 7: ... but the scene is interrupted by shots of Bela Lugosi and stampeding buffalo

To an extent the seemingly non-conformist style of *Glen or Glenda* can be attributed to its existence as an exploitation film. That is, it belongs to a strand of filmmaking that had minimal concern for narrative coherence or continuity, which regularly used substantial proportions of stock footage and which was not overly concerned with narrative cohesion. Yet *Glen or Glenda* is a different exploitation film from *Maniac*; its didactic intent provides an overarching design. In the more random *Maniac*, intertitles such as the one about 'dementia praecox' are interruptions, designed to provide a veneer of scientific justification to the maniacal events acted out on screen but actually serving only to add to the film's bewildering nature. In contrast, the voice-over explanations in *Glen or Glenda* are, with the exception of one section, used throughout the film in a way that indicates the film's serious intent. The low budget, and the traditions of the exploitation film, explains the extensive use of stock footage, though Wood's aspirations as a filmmaker also provide a plausible explanation for the periodic reliance on visual stylisation. *Glen or Glenda* is less avant-garde than a film that seems to be striving towards art and a message, wherein lies both its failure and disarming sincerity.

The exception to the film's overall cohesion comes in the sequence after Barbara has accepted Glen's marriage proposal. The voice-over disappears to make way for a series of scenes apparently dramatising Glen's fears of what would happen if Barbara discovers his secret transvestism. The documentary drama format gives way to a clear, if amateurish attempt at stylisation: acute angles, extreme close-up, superimpositions, theatrical gestures, the appearance of the devil. At least in some versions, in the middle of all this are a series of shots of burlesque dancers, as well as whipping and bondage scenes, intercut with occasional shots of Glen and the Scientist. This is the added footage to which Weiss referred, and which was presumably inserted not just to extend the film's length but to offer the risqué material that an exploitation audience expected. In fact, these sequences add considerably to the bewildering nature of the film.

This footage has been traced to an unidentified film directed by Merle Connell (see Grey 1995: 198), whose filmmaking career offers an interesting comparison with that of Wood. Like Wood, Connell worked on exploitation films with Weiss, directing *Test Tube Babies*. He worked almost entirely within the exploitation field, setting up his own company, Quality Pictures, and operating Quality Studios, which was where Wood shot *Plan 9 from Outer Space*. Schaefer describes him as 'one of the most prolific and professional of the peep producers' (1999: 306), responding to the way the Second World War period had brought about increased possibilities for the display of the female body by developing a business based on short films of burlesque dancers. He moved into features with films such as *The Devil's Sleep* (1949) and *The Flesh Merchant* (1956). These have a 'wages of sin' narrative and a tableaux filming style that doesn't move that far from the approach Connell adopted for filming a striptease artist such as Lili St Clair. Thus, in *The Flesh Merchant* (also known as *The Wild and the Wicked*) 22-year-old Nancy arrives in Hollywood seeking a good time, ignores the warning of her big sister Paula, and moves from working as an 'art class' model into a prostitution racket. In a speech delivered at the end of the film, Paula turns on the women and men, denouncing 'girls who have nothing to sell but their bodies', the drunks and lechers who buy them, and the flesh merchant who runs the operation. This self-critique follows earlier scenes which hint at but deny frontal nudity. Connell's *Untamed Women* (1952) is slightly different. Its narrative of American pilots stranded on a South Sea island occupied by spear-carrying female Druids moves away from the boarding houses and brothels of *The Flesh Merchant*. Its extensive use of stock footage includes prehistoric monsters from *One Million B.C.* (1940) and the almost obligatory volcano eruption, but it retained a focus on women in semi-revealing outfits. It reached the heights of a double-bill with *Bela Lugosi Meets a Brooklyn Gorilla* (1952) and a surprisingly respectable review in the *Los Angeles Times* (see G. K. 1952).

Cornell's *Not Tonight, Henry* (1960) was, along with Russ Meyer's *The Immoral Mr Teas* (1959), a sign of a shift in the exploitation market. It was described in the press as both 'America's first art comedy' (Anon. 1960: B8) and one of a series of 'cheap, plotless pantomimes' that brought nudity to American cinemas (Schumark 1960: 51). It was a relatively elaborate, colour production in which comedian Hank Henry played the husband who escapes from marital drudgery by day-dreaming of being Napoleon and other historical figures and meeting a succession of semi-clad or topless women. At the end of this pantomime (lacking spoken dialogue, the dreams rely on the explanatory voice-over of sexologist Dr Finster) he returns to his now amenable and negligee-clad wife who, asked if he needs to sleep on the couch again, replies, 'Not tonight, Henry', turning the film's title into a statement of marital compliance rather than denial. As Schaefer notes, while in some respects the material resembled what might have been a sketch on a television show of the era, the film's nudity and innuendo differentiated it from both television and other forms cinema (2012: 300). Connell himself reported that it encountered trouble from the police but not the courts (see Schumark 1960: 51). He operated on the edge of the permissible, generally outside the Hollywood sphere in terms of content but also style. He was a more anonymous, less ambitious and, within his field, more successful figure than Wood. He has never been a cult figure but is more representative of

one strand of American cinema, if also home viewing, in the 1950s and
into the 1960s.

Conclusion

Taking a relatively long view of trash cinema reveals that the characteristics identified in the second half of the twentieth century were also
present in the first. The cult of the low and the 'bad' was evident in 1930s
America, a decade when the dominance of classical Hollywood needs to
be seen alongside other filmmaking practices that placed less emphasis
on narrative coherence and the values of the well-made play and more
on action, spectacle and thrills. Where attention has been paid to earlier
examples of trash cinema or filmmakers the tendency has been to treat
them as isolated instances or marginal figures, just as the cult of Edward
D. Wood Jr. has often been based on his outsider status. The validity of
this in the case of Wood should be set against a broader historical context of competing demands within a layered institutional framework and
hierarchy of values. Our understanding of 1930s Hollywood is coloured by
the industry's own discourses that emphasised the 'better' picture and
the universal acceptability of the films of the major studios. This image
was promoted as a response to reformers and critics whose starting point
could be that trash cinema was a tautology. Other images offer different
pictures, based on melodrama, sensation and exploitation.

Twenty years ago Paul Watson urged that 'The schema according to
which exploitation cinema is distinguished from the institution and history of cinema should be abandoned, and attention turned to the histo-
riographic, aesthetic and economic discursive structures through which
all cinema operates. All these areas of practice contribute fundamentally
to the recognition that *all* cinema is, to a greater or lesser extent, exploitation cinema (1997: 81–2). Watson's comments formed part of a larger
argument about the relationship between film theory and historiography
and contemporary film practices but it is useful to bear in mind his particular point about the centrality of exploitation to commercial cinema
in general. In the 1930s, 1940s and 1950s it was both a core element to
Hollywood and an area of cinema that existed beyond Hollywood and
even beyond Poverty Row. In the latter sense it belonged to a hierarchy
operating through production, distribution and exhibition. That hierarchy

was remarkably resilient across those decades. It allowed for a degree of border-crossing, as the status of individual films shifted in response to reception or their distance from their original release, and where the tastes of audiences varied. It also led to the identification of varieties of trash cinema not as a characterisation of cinema in its entirety but as a ways of making distinctions within cinema.

The picture had shifted by the 1950s, by which time the B-film had become an even less clear-cut category, when divisions within Hollywood's audience were becoming more apparent, and when independent production had taken on a new importance. They were changing again at the start of the 1960s, with films such as *Not Tonight, Henry* and other shifts in exploitation filmmaking. For exploitation filmmaker Barry Mahon, interviewed in 1964, 'nudies' such as *Not Tonight, Henry* were different from exploitation films which dealt with 'prostitution, white slavery, adultery, and anything that might fall into the category of sex', and which could play to as many women in the auditorium as men (quoted in Hitchens 1964: 1–2). Yet Mahon admitted that the nudie tended to be defined as a form of exploitation cinema, 'because the advertising generally over-sells what you see when you get inside' (Hitchens 1964: 1). In a sense, trash was becoming more visible while cinema's longstanding tradition of hucksterism was maintained, in the low and not so low reaches of the American film industry. It was in this context that a more specific trash film aesthetic emerged.

3   TRASH AESTHETICS

In 1976 John Russell Taylor wrote of visiting the Nuart, 'West Los Angeles home of the trash movie – *Pink Flamingos* [1972] plays there at midnight every Saturday, *Thundercrack* [1975] every Friday, and should you happen to have missed *The Texas Chainsaw Massacre* [1974] or *Tunnelvision* [1976] or *Mondo Trasho* [1969] you can pick them up scattered among Orson Welles and Bette Davis and Woody Allen' (1976–77: 37). For Taylor, the trash movie, ranging as it did from *Beware! The Blob* (1972) to *The Merchant of Four Seasons* (1972), occupied 'a *terrain vague*, not exactly commercial, not exactly underground, not exactly pornographic, but a bit of all. There is an element of deliberate defiance about them. Some films are trash by accident; these are trash by design' (ibid.). Taylor discovered this deliberate trash in 'films that not only do not claim to be art, but resolutely claim not to be' (ibid.). They rejected not only Hollywood conventions but also the visual pleasures or intellectual demands of art cinema and the avant-garde.

Taylor might have used another name. In *Midnight Movies*, for instance, J. Hoberman and Jonathan Rosenbaum (1991) discuss the trend in filmmaking and the film performance, particularly based in New York but spreading to other metropolitan centres, spanning Underground cinema of the 1960s, the early films of John Waters and David Lynch, and the edges of exploitation cinema and later avant-garde developments. However, Taylor's references to trash, and trash by design, are significant.

Trash had long been used as a term of rejection and condemnation; its explicit celebration by audiences and adoption by filmmakers was a distinctive development of the 1960s and 1970s.

This chapter looks at that development. Having examined films viewed as trash, and the hierarchies operating within the film industry, it shall move on to films that were explicitly designed as trash, and the development of a trash aesthetic. First we shall look at the period up to 1970 and the release that year of the Paul Morrissey-directed film called *Trash*, looking at the art of trash within American Underground cinema of the 1960s. Thus the concern here is not with *Blood Feast* (1963), *Faster, Pussycat! Kill! Kill!* (1965), *A Thousand Pleasures* (1968) or other 1960s films that could be seen as deliberately cultivating a trash style within exploitation cinema. In moving on to John Waters as a filmmaker who came out of Underground scene we shall look at someone who drew on the avant-garde and the exploitation film, and who more than anyone else promoted a trash aesthetic, within and beyond his films. Finally, in bringing this discussion closer to the present, we shall consider what a trash aesthetic means in term of visual imagery, as well as differences between what we might call high and low trash. The discussion of Guy Maddin's *The Forbidden Room* (2015) is in line with the overall concern of this chapter, but comparing this with Robert Rodriguez's *Planet Terror* (2007) provides an opportunity to examine different uses of digital imagery to construct the look of decayed film, and to gain a perspective on the relationship between the arthouse and the grindhouse trash aesthetic.

Thus a contradiction between films that resolutely claim not to be art and the art of trash is at the heart of this discussion. Jack Stevenson put it one way when he wrote of trash as a new aesthetic, one that transformed an insulting, dismissive term into 'a rebellion against the hypocrisy, fascism and elitism of art and a glorification of all things anti-art, of the transparently cheap' (2003: 125). For Stevenson, trash was a thoroughly American invention, scorning European conceptualist art, deifying the thing rather than the meaning of the thing, ignoring the creator's philosophy, intention or politics: 'It spurns the highbrow culture of art criticism (a virus transplanted from Europe) and is itself impervious to criticism. If you dismantle it, there is nothing there' (ibid.). Founded on an appreciation of low-budget, commercial B-films of the 1950s and 1960s, for Stevenson trash emerged as a style at a precise point in time: in 1963 with Jack

Smith's *Flaming Creatures*, a film that was 'one hundred percent trash, shot on trash film stock, populated with the social outcasts "trash" of society, and permeated at every pass with the cluttered, crumbling decay that Smith loved to wallow in' (2003: 126).

Rather than setting art against trash, this sets one image of art against another. The trash aesthetic of Jack Smith and others can be better seen as a rebellion against the elitism of art rather than against art itself, a rejection of the distinction between the avant-garde and kitsch along with a rejection of the norms (but not the allure) of classical Hollywood. The art of trash has a European as well as an American history. It includes Vincent Van Gogh's 'Today I went to visit the place where the dustmen dump the garbage. Lord, how beautiful it is' (quoted in Hauser 2002: 42) and Kurt Schwitters' 'I don't see why one shouldn't use in a picture, just as one uses colours made by the paint merchants, things like old tram and train tickets, scraps of driftwood, cloakroom tickets, ends of string, bicycle wheel stokes – in a word all the things which you find in dustbins or on a rubbish heap' (quoted in Whiteley 2011: 87). Making a different use of the metaphor of the virus, for Gillian Whiteley 'the use of trash as a raw material for art-making is currently not just preponderant: it is endemic' (2011: 151). Here, however, my concern is with the particular American film history of the use of trash and the creation of trash, mainly but not exclusively in the 1960s and 1970s.

From East of Borneo to Trash

It is useful to begin again in the 1930s. Universal's *East of Borneo* (1931) is a curious jungle melodrama, the end result of troubled location shooting, an evidently unhappy star (Rose Hobart), combined with a Sadean narrative that has shades of *The Most Dangerous Game* (1932). It might be all but forgotten now but for the fact that the reclusive American surrealist, Joseph Cornell, acquired a print of the film. Cornell was developing the art of assemblage, collecting junk (from then generally despised Victoriana or Hollywood publicity images) and using this in carefully constructed boxes that he made into works of art. Using some of the same principles on the film he had acquired, Cornell removed the original *East of Borneo* soundtrack along with other material that might have left a discernible narrative and that didn't feature the film's lead. He re-edited the footage and inserted shots from other, unidentified films. Cornell's passion was for silent cinema, and when he projected what he had created he slowed the film down to 'silent speed', used a colour filter as if he was showing a tinted print, and provided an assortment of Latin American music as accompaniment to Hollywood's image of the Far East. The result was *Rose Hobart*, shown to a small circle of artists in the 1930s and following decades, and then in the 1960s elevated to a key work of American avant-garde cinema, an early example of the found footage film. 'Trash' is a potentially misleading word to describe a film that is a loving tribute but also a denial of Hollywood narrative, with shots mismatched or cut short before their narrative significance can become apparent. However, Cornell's use of discarded Hollywood orientalism has a place in this narrative both for its early transformation of existing, worn-out footage into art and for being one of the films that interested Jack Smith and Ken Jacobs, members of a new avant-garde generation who started to make films in the 1950s and who came to prominence in the 1960s.

The broader context to this was the intersection of different forms of cinephilia, writing on cinema and artistic experimentation that converged in downtown New York, that took on a particular significance at the end of the 1950s and the beginning of the 1960s. Established in 1955 by Jonas Mekas, the journal *Film Culture* played a particularly important role in this, in the way in which it combined debates on American avant-garde filmmaking but also on cinema more generally. The eclectic enthusiasm of Mekas led him to write in his diary: '(28 June 1962) I have almost unlimited taste! I can enjoy the poetry of Brakhage, the silent movies of Griffith and Eisenstein, the movies of Hawks and Ulmer, the pornographic flicks of Hobokin, the films of Vanderbeek, the psychiatric movies shown at Cinema 16, the Westerns shown only on 42nd Street, and, depending on my mood, practically anything that moves on screen' (2016: 68) A similar eclecticism is illustrated in the Winter 1962/63 issue of *Film Culture*, which included contributions from Andrew Sarris, Manny Farber, Pauline Kael and Jack Smith, and material on topics ranging from the films of experimental artist Robert Breer to Orson Welles' 1938 *War of the Worlds* radio broadcast.

The Sarris and Farber essays were themselves different responses to films previously regarded as having little value. In 'Notes on the Auteur Theory in 1962', Sarris set out the three premises of the auteur theory, making the case for technical competence, the distinguishable person-ality of the director, and the interior meaning created from the tension between directorial personality and material as the means of raising the status of the Hollywood auteur. In 'White Elephant Art vs. Termite Art', Farber set out a critique of what he identified as the masterpiece/white elephant art that had come to dominate television and cinema, swamp-ing everything with ravishing technique. Against this, he praised the ter-mite art of Howard Hawks and William Faulkner's work on *The Big Sleep* (1946) that had 'no ambitions towards gilt culture', and argued that, 'The best examples of termite art appear in places other than films, where the spotlight of culture is nowhere in evidence' (1998: 135, 136). Sarris and Farber represented what Sarris was later to describe as 'the second underground thing. It was the perception that a great many things that were considered disreputable, grubby, cheap, vulgar, were really much more interesting than that' (quoted in Stanfield 2011: 220). Smith, and his essay 'The Perfect Filmic Appositeness of Maria Montez', came from what Sarris described as the genuine Underground, a world of subversive ideas, 'either political or social, or sexual, or behavioural, or formal, or artistic' (ibid.).

Like Sarris, Jack Smith understood film as a visual rather than a liter-ary medium, as 'a thing of light and shadows' (1997: 33) he wrote in his *Film Culture* contribution. Like Farber, Sarris and Mekas he was suspicious of the growing respectability of European art film: 'At this moment there is a general feeling of movies being approved of' (1997: 28), he complained. In other respects, his essay has little in common with the others pub-lished in *Film Culture*. It is a fan letter, written in celebration of what he described as a

> gaudy array of secret-flix ... Judy Canova flix (I don't even remember the names), *I Walked with a Zombie*, *White Zombie*, *Hollywood Hotel*, all Montez flix, most Dorothy Lamour sarong flix, a gem called *Night Monster*, *Cat & the Canary*, *The Pirate*, Maureen O'Hara Spanish Galleon flix (all Spanish galleon flix anyway), all Busby Berkeley flix, *Flower Thief*, all musicals that had production numbers, espe-cially Rio de Janeiro prod. nos., all Marx Bros. flix... (1997: 32)

For Smith such films, and in particular *Cobra Woman* (1944) and other films starring Maria Montez, should be celebrated for their very phoniness, for phoniness 'could be valued as rich in interest and revealing' (1997: 33). Cornell's devotion to Hollywood stars such as Rose Hobart and Hedy Lamarr distinguished them from their material: of Lamarr, Cornell wrote, 'Amongst screw-ball comedy and the most superficial brand of clap-trap drama, she yet manages to retain a depth and dignity that enables her to enter this world of expressive silence' (quoted in Sitney 1990: 73). For Smith, in contrast, the clap-trap was essential to what he loved. It did not matter if the acting was lousy: 'if something genuine got on film why carp about acting – which HAS to be phony anyway – I'd RATHER HAVE atrocious acting' (1997: 34). Defending the Dominican star against the accusation that she was 'the World's Worst actress' and that her films were 'juvenile ... trash', his answer was that 'juvenile does not equal shameful and trash is the material of creators. ... Trash is true of Maria Montez flix but so are jewels' (1997: 27).

In singing the praises of Maria Montez, Smith was not celebrating a B-movie star but a one-time celebrity whose roles had included films such as *Arabian Nights* (1942), Universal's first all-colour feature, a film that broke opening-day records and helped to make its producer, Walter Wanger, the second-highest paid man in Hollywood. Smith's other contribution to *Film Culture* was on Josef von Sternberg, a filmmaker equally associated with visual extravagance but also with the prestige Paramount picture. Smith's affection for films such as *I Walked with a Zombie* and *Night Monster* (1942) reveals an interest in the high end of the B-film, but alongside the A-list kitsch of Spanish galleon films, as well as the more avant-garde pleasures of Ron Rice's *Flower Thief* (1960). In this context, Montez films existed as trash and jewels on account of their spectacle unrestrained by tastefulness and the way in which they had become part of the detritus of Hollywood. No longer revived by neighbourhood cinemas, they were now only viewable on television in abbreviated and butchered versions:

> cut & stabbed & punished. All are now safe from Montez embarrassment – the tiny nabes are torn down, didn't even make supermarkets – the big nabes have to get back investments so can't be asked (who'd ask) to show them. The art houses are committed to seriousness and importance... (1997: 28).

Smith's sulk against seriousness contrasts with Sarris's interest in elevating the previously despised. But Smith was not only a contributor to *Film Culture*. He was a central figure within a group of avant-garde film-makers, as both performer and director. He appeared, cavorting in front of the camera, in films such as Ron Rice's *The Queen of Sheba Meets the Atom Man* (1963), as Batman in Andy Warhol's *Batman Dracula* (1964), and in *Little Stabs at Happiness* and *Blonde Cobra*, both made by Ken Jacobs between 1959 and 1963, the latter from footage by Bob Fleischner. Of *Blonde Cobra* Hoberman and Rosenbaum wrote: 'Smith dressed up in drag or baby clothes, pulverised a radio with a hammer, feasted on clumps of fallen plaster, and burned holes in his friend's necktie. The performance established Smith as an underground star' (1991: 48). Around the same time, Jacobs appeared in Smith's three-minute *Scotch Tape* (1959–62). Jacobs apparently proposed *Revelling in the Dumps* for the title: instead, Smith chose to name the film after the dirty piece of tape that had wedged itself inside the camera gate and was thus visible on the bottom right of the frame throughout the film. Far from attempting to conceal its imperfections, this was filmmaking that drew attention to them.

Smith's fascination with Universal horror films, mixed with a bit of Busby Berkeley, is most evident in the uncompleted *Normal Love* (1963–65), which had earlier gone under various titles, including *Normal Sex*, *The Great Moldy Triumph* and *The Great Patsy Triumph*. He became notorious for the 43-minute *Flaming Creatures* (1963). Filmed on outdated black-and-white stock that gave a washed-out look, *Flaming Creatures* not only lacks a discernible narrative but also, aside from an occasional bared breast or limp penis, a clear sense of the sex of the performers, or even of what is taking place. There is a rape sequence, an earthquake, vampirism, shots of men, women and men dressed as women, dancing or lying on the floor. The camera is hand-held and often shaky, the image often obscure. At one point the Hollywood orientalism and 1960s pop-songs of the soundtrack give way to a fake lipstick commercial which provokes the question, 'Is there a lipstick that doesn't come off when you suck cock?' ('A man is not supposed to have lipstick on his cock' is the prim reply). In the context of the early 1960s it was strikingly transgressive, a film that offended against sexual norms and distinctions with glee. Mekas praised the taboo-shattering film as an example of 'Baudelairean cinema', along with *The Queen of Sheba Meets the Atom Man*, *Blonde Cobra* and *Little*

Stabs at Happiness (see Hoberman and Rosenbaum 1991: 51). The controversy surrounding it culminated in the film's seizure by the New York police and the arrest of Mekas and Jacobs (then acting as projectionist for the screening). The resulting trial led to the conviction of Mekas and Jacobs and the banning of *Flaming Creatures* for obscenity (1991: 60–1).

The combination of camp and trash was evident in other New York Underground films of the 1960s, but in different ways. Like Smith, twin brothers George and Mike Kuchar looked to Hollywood. Given an 8mm camera for their twelfth birthday, they went on to make *The Wet Destruction of the Atlantic Empire* (1954) and similarly absurdly titled films, affectionately parodying Hollywood by relocating its scenarios to their own Bronx neighbourhood and substituting glamorous stars with friends happy to act up and undress in front of the camera. Promoted by Mekas alongside the work of Andy Warhol, Kenneth Anger and others, they moved to 16mm and independent careers for films such as George Kuchar's *Hold Me While I'm Naked* (1966) and Mike Kuchar's *The Sins of the Fleshapoids* (1966).

Hold Me While I'm Naked parodied both Hollywood melodrama and the avant-garde filmmaker. The opening titles proudly announce 'Miss Kerness's clothes by Hope Morris', having already introduced both Donna Kerness and Hope Morris among the stars of the film. The director then interrupts the filming by interjecting, 'Let me just wind up the camera and I think it would be better if you were... Helen, if you would remove the brassiere. The mysticism of the stained glass window and the profanity of the brassiere do not go well together.' Set 'a million years in the future', *The Sins of the Fleshapoids* dramatised human betrayal and the love between two Fleshapoid robots. Here the future is created in overdressed bedrooms and through deliberately primitive drawings, while an earthly paradise is evoked with little more than a bowl of fruit and a chocolate bar. The soundtrack includes sections of Bernard Herrmann's score for *The Seventh Voyage of Sinbad* (1958) while dialogue appears in cartoon bubble form. The Kuchars' disarming celebration of the inept, the kitsch and bodily functions continued beyond the 1960s. It included George's collaboration with Curt McDowell on *Thundercrack!*, a film that mixed 'old dark house' horror, idiosyncratic and extended dialogue and monologues, with hardcore sex: straight, gay and gorilla suit. As such it made it into John Russell Taylor's understanding of the trash movie, occupying a territory between the commercial mainstream, the pornographic and the Underground, establishing a regular place on the midnight circuit and at cinemas such London's Scala.

Other filmmakers exploited the kitsch qualities of popular culture and engaged with sexual diversity in different ways. Kenneth Anger's *Scorpio Rising* (1963) accompanied homoerotic, Christian and fascist imagery with a pop soundtrack ranging from Little Peggy Marsh's 'Wind-Up Doll' to the Crystals' 'He's a Rebel'. In contrast to Anger's Eisensteinian editing, Andy Warhol, for Simon Warner, is 'the king, or indeed queen, of the trash aesthetic' (2014: 45), minimalising personal intervention, making single-shot films with a camera that didn't move and for which the actors were given little or no direction. Warhol (who made an appearance in Smith's *Normal Sex*) turned artistic values on their head, embracing superficiality and emptiness, and rejecting the enduring values of art for the mechanical and the transient. His films, or the films that bore his name, also helped turn the Underground film into something of a commercial enterprise.

Such films initially circulated within a small circle but during the 1960s achieved a higher profile. The censorship problems of *Flaming Creatures* and also *Scorpio Rising* attracted significant press coverage, while Mekas consistently used his *Village Voice* column to promote favoured avant-garde filmmakers. With the multi-screen *Chelsea Girls* (1966) Warhol's films began to attract wider attention, and commercial success, even as Warhol's own contribution became less certain. Paul Morrissey came to play an increasingly important role at Warhol's Factory, taking the films towards a form of narrative coherence and realist depiction. Released under what had effectively become the Warhol brand, the Morrissey-directed *Flesh* (1968), *Trash* (1970) and *Heat* (1972) moved away from the static camera of the earlier films while retaining disdain for any stylistic elaboration in the way they stared at the underside of New York life.

Trash helped to give a name to this trend. For Pauline Kael the title was 'perhaps the cleverest ploy of the movie season. It has the advantage of that self-depreciating humor that makes criticism seem foolish' (1997: 90). Morrissey was equally cynical in suggesting that his intentions were to show that there was 'no difference between a person using drugs and a piece of refuse' (quoted in Davies 2009: 18). Conceived as deglamourised answer to the depiction of drugs found in films such as *Easy Rider* (1969), its title evokes household waste and the junk of the junkie but the film counters critical and even directorial dismissal through the defiance of its performances, in particular Holly Woodlawn as Holly Santiago. In *Trash* the camera is pointed at, and seeks out, the rejected and the damaged, linking garbage with people's lives but also showing the vitality of that world and the use that is made of what has been disposed of by others.

Trash starts as the story of the heroin-addicted Joe Smith (Joe Dallesandro). It becomes equally the story of Holly, his partner, and her determination to adopt her sister's baby so that she can get on welfare. At one point Holly's determination to furnish the place where she and Joe live takes her onto the street, where she finds an abandoned mattress. Joe asks her why she wants a piece of garbage. 'It's not garbage, it's a mattress,' she insists. 'You can use it, you can sleep on it. A mattress is not garbage.' Turning to a pile of wooden drawers, she tells him that they can use these also. Joe calls them 'a piece of shit' but this only makes Holly even more excited: 'Shit! How can you call this shit! Look at this, this is gold, gold-plated.' Holly's determination not to accept the values imposed by others is reinforced by her camp performance, her wild gestures contrasting with the impassivity of Joe Dallesandro. This is not the naïve camp of the transvestism presented in *Glen or Glenda*, which has invited camp readings because of its failed seriousness.

Born Haroldo Santiago Franceschi Rodriquez Danhakl, Holly Woodlawn brought her own transvestite life into the film in the form of what Chuck Kleinhans called 'deliberate low Camp' – though he also uses the word trash – based in the perception that taste, aesthetic sensibility and sexu-

Fig. 8: Holly scavenges among the trash in *Trash*

ality are socially constructed (1993: 189). Holly's insistence on the gold-plated nature of junk also provides a link, as Jon Davies notes, with what Jack Smith identified in Maria Montez, an extraordinary self-belief, in herself and her role, one that was genuine in its very artifice (2009: 152).

John Waters

By 1970 trash existed as a film title, the characters and world it portrayed and (despite itself) valued, and more generally as an aesthetic that was becoming increasingly visible. By this time exploitation cinema was developing its own trash aesthetic, leading Randy Palmer to write of Hershell Gordon Lewis, director of *Blood Feast* (1963): 'He's never pretended to be something other than what he is. He *knows* his movies are trash, and he'll be the first to admit it with a twinkle in his eye' (2006: 7). Exploitation cinema continued to justify its sensationalism in *Mondo* films that used the documentary form to show extreme images but films such as Lewis's *Scum of the Earth* (1963) insisted on their grubby qualities even before its director moved into delivering this in lurid detail.

Even the Hollywood majors were accused – in John Simon's review of the British-made, Warner Bros.-funded *Performance* (1970) – of supporting what Simon called 'the Loathsome Film', a European and American trend, also including *Barbarella* (1967), *Dillinger is Dead* (1968), *Boom* (1968), *Secret Ceremony* (1968), *Candy* (1968), *End of the Road* (1970), *Something for Everyone* (1970), *Myra Breckinridge* (1970) and *Beyond the Valley of the Dolls* (1970). Picking up on this attack *Myra Breckinridge* director Michael Sarne wrote to the *New York Times* welcoming Simon's accusation. He argued that, 'The Loathsome Film (an excellent title, and one I hope you will hang on to) is an attempt to reflect artistically what is happening to the world socially' (Sarne 1970: 14; see also Benshoff 2008). Thus, the dismissive label was adopted with pride.

Taste, genre and often gender boundaries were being tested in films made by major Hollywood studios, leaving many critics unsure of how to respond. For the filmmaker, a negative comment could be just as welcome as a positive one. Thus, in his account of the reception of *Pink Flamingos*, John Waters lists the favourable reviews in *New York* magazine and *Interview*, but highlights in particular the headline given to the delayed *Variety* review:

DREGS OF HUMAN PERVERSITY
DRAWS WEIRDO ELEMENT.
MONSTROUS (1991: 21)

Waters was the filmmaker who more than anyone accepted 'trash' as to be celebrated rather than denied. 'I devoted all my time to the exploration of cinematic garbage,' he wrote of his early interest in cinema. 'At last I had a goal in life – I wanted to make the trashiest motion pictures in cinema history' (1991: 34). *The Roman Candles* (1966), his first short film, was promoted (with a nod towards the multi-screen *Chelsea Girls*) as 'a triple projected trash epic', though of *Eat Your Makeup* (1968), the third and last of his early short films, he wrote, 'I hadn't really found the trashy look and subject matter that made my later films successful' (1991: 54). *Mondo Trasho* (1969), the title of his next film and first feature, evoked trash and the sensationalist Mondo documentaries, as well as Russ

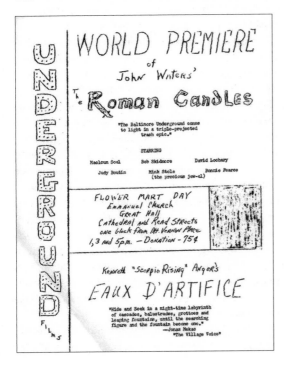

Fig. 9: Flier for
Roman Candles

Meyer's *Mondo Topless* (1966). It was promoted as 'a gutter film' and, in the *Provincetown Advocate* 'an underground epic of all that is trashy in life'. He has described the best review he ever got as an essay by David Chute that 'ended with this supreme compliment: "In *Desperate Living* Waters comes close to creating a work of true trash art"' (1991: 177).

The trash label has also been regularly adopted in commentary on his films, from Steve Yeager's 1998 documentary, *Divine Trash*, to the 'Genuine Trash' essay provided with the 2017 Blu-ray release of *Multiple Maniacs* (1970). In interviews and articles Waters has been sceptical about labels such as camp and cult, for instance commenting that, 'They always refer to my films as cult movies and I'm never quite sure what they mean' (1991: 214). However, the collection of writings published as *Crackpot: The Obsessions of John Waters*, was promoted with the endorsement of William S. Burroughs that 'John Waters is the Pope of Trash and his taste in tacky is unexcelled'. Subsequent press stories on Waters have tended to repeat the 'Pope of Trash' label, or to use headings such as 'John Waters Talks Trash' (*Sight & Sound*, September 2015).

In his films Waters drew on the avant-garde and exploitation. He has identified his filmmaking heroes as William Castle, Hershell Gordon Lewis (*Multiple Maniacs* acknowledged Lewis's *Two Thousand Maniacs!* [1964]) and Russ Meyer, for their showmanship and exploitation of gore and sex. Combining these different strands, he has also written that underneath all his posing 'as a trash film enthusiast, a little known fact is that I actually sneak off in disguise (and hope to God I'm not recognized) to arty films in the same way business men rush in to see *Pussy Talk* on their lunch hour' (1986: 108). In fact, taking inspiration from naked commercialism and cinema at its least commercial, and from the low and the high, seems central to both the films and the persona he has constructed. For Waters is a key figure within trash cinema as both a filmmaker and a personality. At the time of writing, he has not made a theatrical-release film since *A Dirty Shame* (2004). His presence has been more evident elsewhere, through his one-man show *This Filthy World* and the documentary made of it in 2006, interviews, talks, commentaries and further books: *Role Models* (2010), *Carsick: John Waters Hitchhikes Across America* (2014) and *Make Trouble* (2017).

His early films take clear inspiration from the New York Underground. In particular he learnt from the willingness to flout convention, challenge taboos and bend sexual norms. As he put it, 'the Kuchar brothers gave me the self-confidence to believe in my own tawdry vision' (quoted in Bergan 2011). The desire to shock came partly from the avant-garde but also from exploitation cinema and a sense of showmanship, most clearly evident in the speech that Mr David (David Lochary) delivers at the start of *Multiple Maniacs*:

> Yes, folks, this isn't any cheap X-rated movie or fifth-rate porno play, this is the show you want: Lady Divine's cavalcade of perversions, the sleaziest show on earth. Not actors, not paid imposters, but real actual filth who have been carefully screened in order to present to you the most flagrant violation of natural law known to man.

This, then, was not just filmmaking about the low-life or made cheaply. It was cinema promoted as trash, perversity and filth.

To call something filth is, of course, to say more than that it is disposable. While one understanding of trash is as something lacking in value, filth signifies a negative value, something that is unclean or obscene. Its adoption was in part a response to censorship, turning an accusation into something to be celebrated. Including 'two actual queers kissing' in the cavalcade of perversions in *Multiple Maniacs* served as a reflection on social norms but the film retains its power to offend in intercutting a nativity scene with simulated anal sex with rosary beads between Divine and the self-style 'religious whore' (Mink Stole) in a church.

Filth was even more central to Waters' next feature, *Pink Flamingos* (1972), the film that became a mainstay of the Midnight Movie scene

Fig. 10: Connie Marbles competes with Divine for the title of 'the filthiest person alive' in *Pink Flamingos*

through the 1970s. Its narrative is based around a contest for 'the filthiest people alive', a battle that includes Divine being sent a birthday present of a turd by her enemies, the Marbles (Lochary and Stole), whose business consists of kidnapping women who are then raped by their butler, after which their babies are sold to lesbian couples. At the end of the film, the Marbles are captured, tried, tarred and feathered and shot by Divine, now unchallenged as the filthiest person in the world. 'Filth is my politics, filth is my life', she tells the invited press. 'Thanks for the scoop, Divine, next month's sales will be booming', says one of the journalists, leaving Divine and her family to discuss which are the filthiest hairstyles and their plans to visit Boise, Idaho. Most notoriously, for the film's coda, in what Kleinhans describes as a 'classic trash moment in film' (1993: 189), Waters' voice-over announces: 'Watch, as Divine proves that not only is she the filthiest person in the world, she is also the filthiest actress in the world. What you are about to see is the real thing.' To the sound of 'How Much is That Doggy in the Window', Divine stoops down to pick up freshly deposited dog shit, puts it in her mouth, grins, chews, and spits it out.

Setting out his philosophy at the beginning of *Shock Value*, Waters wrote:

> To me, bad taste is what entertainment is all about. If someone vomits watching one of my films, it's like getting a standing ovation. But one must remember that there is such a thing as good bad taste and bad bad taste. It's easy to disgust someone; I could make a ninety-minute film of people getting their limbs hacked off, but this would only be bad bad taste and not very stylish or original. To understand bad taste one must have very good taste. Good bad taste can be creatively nauseating but must, at the same time, appeal to the especially twisted sense of humor, which is anything but universal. (1991: 2)

Or, as Jack Stevenson put it, 'Trash ain't Garbage' (2003: 125–30). Waters distinguishes his films as tasteless but stylish comedies, satires and parodies. The infamous final *Pink Flamingos* scene works through showing 'the real thing' (a single take from canine defecation to human consumption) but avoids being scatological pornography through Divine's self-conscious performance and the ironical effect of the soundtrack. The combination of disgusting bad taste and the film's kitsch bad taste (from those trailer trash flamingos to 'How Much is That Doggy in the Window') help to create a knowing and self-conscious trash aesthetic rather than simply trash.

The 'good' of Waters' 'good bad taste' has been evident through humour but in other ways as well. His films moved towards narrative coherence. His first feature, *Mondo Trasho*, is essentially a series of scenes linked by little more than the pop music soundtrack. Mr David's plot to murder Lady Divine gives *Multiple Maniacs* an overarching narrative but this contains extensive digressions (notably the nativity scenes) and moments when any logic is abandoned (as when Lady Divine, having killed other key characters, is raped by a giant, cooked lobster). From *Pink Flamingos* onwards, Waters' films had clear stories, with something akin to good and bad characters (Divine's loving, though albeit murderous, family contrasting with the evil Marbles). Production values increased, particularly in post-Divine films such as *Hairspray* (1988), *Cry-Baby* (1990) and *Serial Mom* (1994), the latter film starring mainstream actors, Kathleen Turner and Sam Waterston. Moving into the mainstream, Waters' films retained a self-conscious awareness of his rebellious but enterprising, Baltimore roots. Thus, in *Pecker* (1998) Edward Furlong plays Pecker, a Baltimore teenage photographer who promotes his work by plastering flyers around the neighbourhood and then finds himself adopted by New York intelligentsia before returning to the more familiar Baltimore. As Walter Metz observes (2003: 164), Pecker is clearly a version (but not a portrayal) of Waters both in his particular behaviour (Waters promoted his early films in a similar way) and in being caught between the conflicting demands of local but obscure integrity (and trash) and the moderated respectability of wider fame.

The Forbidden Room and Planet Terror

The 2017 Blu-ray reissue of Waters' *Multiple Maniacs* caused the dvdbeaver reviewer to note that the film

> was shot in 16mm but looks beautifully rich with grain on this is [sic] dual-layered disc sporting a max'ed out bitrate. Contrast is wonderful, although scenes with an abundance of white can look

> blown-out. There are some irregularities that seem appropriate to
> the original production. Still, I was genuinely impressed with the
> visuals and I can't image the film, even initially, ever looking this
> strong. There is minor depth but no noise and this representation
> has consistent and finely supported grain structure. (Tooze 2017)

However, while one effect of digitalisation has been physically (thankfully
not morally) to clean up the grain of Waters' early films, and to restore
other examples of low-cost trash from *Manos: The Hands of Fate* upwards,
another has been to enable contemporary filmmakers to approximate and
exceed the distressed look of earlier films. This is evident in *Death Proof*
and *Planet Terror*, Quentin Tarantino's and Robert Rodriguez's respective
contributions to *Grindhouse*, their 2007 tribute to 1970s exploitation
films, and in retrosploitation films that followed on from the Tarantino/
Rodriguez films such as *Hobo with a Shotgun* (2011).

Guy Maddin's *The Forbidden Room* offers a different but equally distressed look, and draws on different material. Maddin's films are known
for the ways in which they invoke silent cinema, accentuating a melodra-
matic style far beyond anything evident in the films they evoke. For David
Church, Maddin's work is 'not a celebration of exploitation or "trash"
cinema (as is so much of contemporary cult film), but rather a memorial
to more "legitimate" film styles that have been discarded by history' and
mainstream audiences (2009: 11). Yet asked if his films might be considered 'highbrow melodrama', Maddin's reply was that he did not see much
distinction: 'The goosebump-ometer is just as great for Ed Wood or Paul
Morrissey movies or George Kuchar films as it is for Max Ophüls ... sometimes. And then, as a matter of fact, if it was a tie, the tiebreaker goes
to the trash. To me, it's just more fun' (quoted in Juzwiak 2015). In their
own way, Rodriguez and Maddin have developed a trash aesthetic, using
digital doctoring and performance style. Examining *The Forbidden Room*
and *Planet Terror* provides an opportunity to examine different aspects of
twenty-first-century digital trash aesthetics.

The Forbidden Room originated in two installations, one at the Centre
Pompidou in Paris, the other at the Phi Centre in Montreal, in which
Maddin, his cast and crew, had the brief to shoot a film a day in full public
view. This then developed into *Seances*, an online project based on lost
movies: films that no longer survived or had never been completed. *The*

Forbidden Room was constructed out of these restaged fragments, which were woven together to create a single feature film, though the narrative remains resolutely episodic. In turn the *Seances* online project allows viewers to create a short film from this material, which can be viewed only once before it disappears.

In *The Forbidden Room*, the supposed recreation of the Dwain Esper sexploitation short, *How to Take a Bath* (1937), serves as something of a framing device, initially leading into a segment about four men trapped in a submarine, their captain missing. The surprise appearance of a woodsman then leads into a narrative about four men in a forest, trying to rescue a kidnapped woman. The woodsman finds Margot, the kidnapped woman, in Mergel's Cave, but cannot rescue her before completing a succession of trials: finger snapping, offal piling, etc. When Margot does escape, alone, it is through the doorway of a dream, where she turns into amnesiac flower girl... These and other incomplete and interlaced stories are set in an exotic landscape featuring trains that travel from Berlin to Bogota and a volcano (which becomes 'valcano' in the silent cinema-style inter-titles) that would not be out of place in *East of Borneo* (or *Rose Hobart*). Towards the close, the woodsman comes across a 'Book of Climaxes' in the submarine, leading to a succession of delirious cliffhanging scenes that reimagine sensationalist cinema and the silent chapter ending as surreal absurdities, from figures falling from buildings to a couple stranded at sea, the woman pointing across the water to a gigantic brain on the horizon, which then explodes when a bomb is dropped from a passing plane. The narrative structure owes a debt to the writings of Raymond Roussel, and his practice of constructing stories through often tangential associations.

The imagery is striking. As in other films, the visual splendour of silent cinema is repeatedly evoked, though as Steven Shaviro wrote of Maddin's earlier work, the result 'is not so much to imitate films from the 1920s as it is to replicate the stereotypical ideas we have about such films now' (2002: 218). This involves an exaggerated performance style, accentuating the melodrama far beyond that evident in films actually made in the 1920, but in *The Forbidden Room* also a deliberate look of deterioration, using the work of Evan Johnson (credited as co-director) and Galen Johnson (production and sound designer). In the 1960s Jack Smith retained the blot left by the piece of scotch tape that had become wedged in the camera

Fig. 11: The look of
aged and decayed
celluloid in *The
Forbidden Room*

Fig. 11: The look of aged and decayed celluloid in *The Forbidden Room*

gate and was happy to use outdated, black-and-white film stock. In *The Forbidden Room* the digital film is deliberately treated to make it appear damaged, aged and unstable. This visual instability is linked to the use of lost films as source material, and a repeated narrative concern with amnesia, bereavement, injury.

The distressed look is applied more selectively to *Planet Terror*. In the film's deliberately formulaic narrative, a toxic chemical leak from a Texas military base leads to go-go dancer Cherry Darling and friends fighting a battle with the zombies unleashed by the leak and the corrupt military from the base. The film's hyper-violence is clearly identified as a reference to earlier exploitation cinema, a point accentuated though its initial presentation alongside Tarantino's *Death Proof* as a part of a double-bill, complete with fake movie trailers for (then) non-existent films. As Nick James put it, the concept of Rodriguez and Tarantino 'was to offer you a full night's B-movie entertainment, a nostalgist's return to the fleapit aesthetics of 1970s cinema trash' (2007: 16). The aesthetics include scratches and marks on the film, and a missing reel that follows a steamy sex scene, the screening of which seemingly causes the film to burn and the projector to jam. The effect is to draw attention to the artificial narrative construction while also (as in *The Forbidden Room*) providing a digitalised illusion of analogue decay and fallibility.

Both *Planet Terror* and *The Forbidden Room* offer nostalgic images of cinema history, one based on 1970s grindhouse cinema, the other on earlier melodrama. The material used ranges from *Der Janus-Kopf* (1920), F. W. Murnau's lost version of *Dr Jekyll and Mr Hyde* staged for *The Forbidden Room*, to a *Women in Cages* (1971) trailer, watched on television

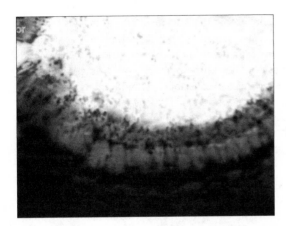

Fig. 12: The look of
burning celluloid
in *Planet Terror*

in *Planet Terror*. The films inhabit very different contexts, but the melodrama of *The Forbidden Room* might be better described as legitimised
rather than legitimate. Reviewing the films, Tony Rayns wrote that Maddin
and Johnson might 'be conjuring vanished films back to life, and lament-
ing the fragility and transience of the medium that sired them, but they
are also into the trashiness of trash culture: the shoddiness of B-movie
effects, overripe ham performances and the kind of tacky glamour that
floated Jack Smith's boat when he made *Flaming Creatures*' (2016: 69).
Trash has come to belong in the arthouse as much as in the grindhouse.

Conclusion

In this chapter I have distinguished between a trash aesthetic and trash
as a more general label applied to films or groups of films. This is to adopt
a narrower approach than the overall emphasis on despised forms and
those who don't despise them, evident, for instance, in the anthology
Trash Aesthetics: Popular Culture and Its Audience (Hunter and Kaye 1997:
2). It is to adopt a looser approach than that taken by Simon Warner in his
distinction between trash culture and a trash aesthetic. For Warner:

> even if we may claim that versions of trash culture have subse-
> quently become almost ubiquitous in the capitalist world and
> beyond – in, for example, junk food and junk mail, reality tel-

evision and celebrity obsession, scandal sheets and news-stand pornography, slot machines and stretch limousines – it does not follow that a trash aesthetic, as such, also exists. Rather, for such an aesthetic to establish its presence requires an artist or a movement to knowingly and self-consciously take the materials of a cultural moment and re-conceptualise those materials in such a way that they represent or comment upon that moment. Then, we may argue still further, that authoritative critical voices are then needed to identify and to contextualise what the artist or movement have done... (2014: 47)

Thus George and Mike Kuchar self-consciously took Hollywood material and re-conceptualised it in a way that functioned as commentary. However, I understand this to constitute a trash aesthetic by itself, one which is then open to identification and contextualisation but not dependent upon it.

John Waters has been central to the discussion as someone who has repeatedly expressed what he does in terms of trash, even if this is often though the adoption of the comments others have made on his films. 'Trash aesthetic' is thus not a precise term with a single meaning. It is given one meaning by Matthew Tinkcom when he writes of what Waters 'calls the "trash aesthetic," whereby his work embraces all manner of marginal subjects in his beloved Baltimore – eccentrics, the downright mad, transvestites – and seeks to embrace these figures by sharing in their delight in disregarding customary notions of good taste, normative sexuality, and racial identities' (2002: 157). It takes on different connotations in Jack Stevenson's observation that the 'trash movie aesthetic was found on an appreciation for the low-budget commercial B-films of the fifties and sixties' (2003: 126) and again in Jeffrey Sconce's reference to the trash aesthetic making inroads into mainstream popular taste through the ironic readings promoted by programmes such as *Mystery Science Theater 3000* (1995: 373). Trash has thus been used to refer to the disposal materials of consumer society but also marginalised people, while a trash aesthetic has functioned as networked entertainment as well as a challenge to social norms.

A trash aesthetic can be high as well as low definition, hence my closing comments on different ways in which contemporary filmmakers have digitally created the look of celluloid deterioration. However, the overall focus here has been on the trash aesthetic that emerged within American Underground cinema in the 1960s and that was picked up by Waters, who to some degree combined the different understandings proposed by Tinkcom, Stevenson, Sconce and Warner. That is, Waters' commitment to the marginalised living outside the boundaries of good taste and normative sexuality was combined with a fascination with low cinema and scandal sheets and with a move towards, and adoption by, more mainstream culture.

This focus has emphasised the camp side of trash: its roots in gay and transvestite subcultures, its concern with challenging norms by finding value in trash, and in embracing and accentuating rather than rejecting the kitsch and the trashy. In its concern with 'trash by design' it has emphasised filmmakers who were also film viewers and film fans. As the John Russell Taylor report quoted at the beginning of this chapter indicates, the trash cinema of the 1970s emerged also through how films were shown, seen and discussed. That cult of trash became even more apparent in the years that followed.

4   THE CULT OF TRASH

The second issue of *Sleazoid Express*, dated 2 July 1980, carried two reviews. In the longer one, under the headline 'NOT REVOLTING ENOUGH', Bill Landis complained that the tribe in *Sacrifice!*, playing at the Times Square Theatre, didn't do as many repulsive things as the one in *Carnivorous*. 'The obligatory cannibalism scenes look very phony,' he wrote. 'There are some good repugnant scenes, but not enough.' To the right of this, under the heading 'UNDERGROUND CLASSIC', was a review of Andy Warhol's *Chelsea Girls* (1966), identified as taking Cinéma Vérité to its extreme and at best managing to show the complexity of human personality. 'It's something of an effort to sit through this movie due to its length and boring stretches, but it's still definitely worthwhile,' Landis advised. A shorter piece below this, headed 'ART MEETS TRASH', reported on films by Kenny Scharf, Drew Straub and Keith Haring, with the comment that, 'these videotapes were entertaining, were short enough not to become dull, and lack usual art school pretentions'. At the bottom of the single, photocopied sheet an announcement of coming attractions highlighted screenings of *Trash* and *Flesh* at the Bleeker Street Cinema alongside screenings of the 1979 Canadian serial killer film *Stone Cold Dead*, the 1973 British Gothic horror film *And Now the Screaming Starts* and *Shock Waves*, described by Landis as 'something about Nazi zombies from underwater starring John Carradine and Peter Cushing'.

Sacrifice! was one of a number of titles used for Umberto Lenzi's 1972 film *Il Paese del sesso sevaggio*: others include *Deep River Savages* and *The Man from Deep River*. Like earlier *Mondo* documentaries, it made a dubious appeal to authenticity to justify scenes of violence against humans and animals, and cannibalism, but it inserted these into a narrative of a English photographer captured, physically abused but eventually accepted into a tribe on the Thailand borders. Rejected by the BBFC in Britain, it was subsequently released on video but then fell foul of the 1984 Video Recordings Act. In some countries it received a relatively mainstream release (see Brandum 2016, for details of its Australian exhibition). In Bill Landis and Michelle Clifford's *Sleazoid Express: A Mindtwisting Tour Through the Grindhouse Cinema of Times Square!* it became an example of Eurosleaze shown in Times Square area grindhouses; more specifically, it belonged to the 'cannibal vomitorium genre', 'Italy's most dubious horror achievement', which properly emerged with Ruggero Deodato's 1977 *L'Ultimo mondo cannibal* (also known as *Canivorous*, *Cannibal* or *The Last Survivor*) and reached a peak of sorts with Deodato's *Cannibal Holocaust* (1979) and Lenzi's *Cannibal Ferox* (1980) (also known as *Make Them Die Slowly* and *Woman from Deep River*) (Landis and Clifford 2002: 205–10).

Landis's initial comments on the film were made when *Sleazoid Express* was a singled-typed sheet, distributed free in local stores and clubs. As such it represented a new form of trash celebration, the first of a succession of zines devoted to the horror film and the margins of cinema more generally. There had been earlier fanzines such as Forrest J. Ackermann's *Famous Monsters of Filmland* (published from 1958) while the first issue of *Fangoria* came out in 1979. However, as David Sanjek noted in his survey of the horror fanzine, the cheaply produced publications that appeared in the 1980s differentiated themselves from 'prozines' which were seen to emphasise slick professionalism in their appearance and their subject matter and too often to function as a means of promoting the latest release (2000: 316). In contrast, in the words of Steve Bissette, *Sleazoid Express* and *Gore Gazette* (first published later in 1980) 'flaunted their homemade aspect. They were all written with a punk attitude and they reflected the residue of the punk era of the seventies' (quoted in Szpunar 2013: 29). Other publications emphasised their commitment to trash culture in their titles. Thus *Sleazoid Express* was followed by *Confessions of a Trash Fiend*,

Trash City, Trashola, Trash Compactor (subtitled *The Magazine of Our Disposable Culture*), *Asian Trash Cinema* and *European Trash Cinema*. *Kill Baby* included 'Trashy Movie Reviews', *Imaginator* included 'Video Trash' while *City Morgue* had 'Trash Reviews from Hell'.

By the time that Jeffrey Sconce commented on 'Publications devoted to this "trash" cinema', those publications were changing, as was their subject matter. *Sleazoid Express* had grown in size but ceased publication in 1985, only to be revived as something closer to a fully-fledged magazine in 1999. The publications mentioned by Sconce included *Psychotronic Video, Trashola, Ungawa!, Film Threat, Incredibly Strange Films* and Michael Weldon's *Psychotronic Encylopedia of Film* (1995: 372), a list that indicates the shifting nature of the devotion to trash. *Psychotronic* was a Xeroxed and handwritten zine, first published in 1980, devoted to films shown on television. It led to the *Psychotronic Encylopedia of Film*, which first appeared in paperback in 1983. The quarterly *Psychotronic Video*, which followed in 1989, included reviews and articles on music, books and mainly exploitation films. *Trashola* was set up in 1981 by Jim Morton in San Francisco, as a 'Schlock and Horror Newsletter', but after it ceased publication in 1984 Morton went on to provide much of the material for *Incredibly Strange Films*, one of a series of RE/Search volumes on topics that ranged from science fiction writer J. G. Ballard to porn artist Annie Sprinkles. *Ungawa!* was a British publication which ran from 1989 to 1992. It was edited by Cathal Tohill, and its contributors included Pete Tombs: in 1995, Tohill and Tombs published *Immoral Tales*, their book on European sex and horror films made between 1956 and 1984. The last print edition of *Film Threat* appeared in 1997, though a website was established in 1996. Other publications joined the move online. When *Sleazoid Express* itself appeared in paperback in 2002 it was to look back on an era: the book ends with a lament for the end of the reign of the vintage exploitation film at the Roxy and the more general closing of 42nd Street area grindhouses (2002: 297). More than ten years earlier, Jack Stevenson had written to another fanzine (*Shock Xpress*), complaining that

> Times have changed on the trash film scene. In NYC 42nd Street is in the grave waiting for the lid to be nailed shut, the Metropolitan on 14th is long closed and now the last sacred altar which Bill [Landis] worshipped so fanatically, got shut down by the health

authorities for numerous sex acts. Finally, all the knowledge Bill used to have about obscure films is now in the public realm as you can buy 20 books about it at the nearest bookstore. (1989: 3)

Examining the film fanzine culture and its move into book and online publishing provides an insight into the nature of this late-twentieth-century cult of trash. It can draw out some of the variations within this, variations evident even within a single *Sleazoid Express* sheet: the juxtaposition of Italian cannibal horror and New York Underground experimentation, the Times Square Theatre and Bleeker Street Cinema, downtown Manhattan screenings and a film directed by an Italian about an Englishman in Thailand. Comparing different publications accentuates this. While *Sleazoid Express* reported on what was showing at the grindhouse and New York clubs, *Psychotronic* presented itself as 'New York's weekly illustrated guide to movies on TV – specialising in the obscure, the low-budget and the awful.' In 1985 Craig Ledbetter's *Hi-Tech Terror* announced itself as the first newsletter devoted to horror and science fiction on videocassette and satellite. Later, with *European Trash Cinema* he abandoned US film production entirely, concentrating mainly on Italian horror. *Ungawa!* combined film reports on crime fiction, true crime and pin-up art. These variations in subject matter were accompanied by differences of purpose and tone. The zines ranged from the studious to the supercilious; their titles often reflected, in Sanjek's words, 'an unseemly juvenile fascination with unrespectable and illicit imagery' (2000: 314) and their sarcastic and jocular tone was 'often laced with self-conscious misogyny, racism and sexism' (2000: 319). They could also be devoted to analysis, auteur celebration, archival documentation or pop surrealist juxtapositions. Acknowledging the existence of factions within the paracinematic audience, Sconce essentially treats it as a single community, while Jancovich described cult movies audiences as 'less an internally coherent "taste culture" than a series of frequently opposed and contradictory reading strategies that are defined through a sense of their difference to an equally coherently imagined "normality"' (2002: 315). Accepting Jancovich's point about oppositions and contradictions, my purpose here is to identify key patterns that operate through these.

In looking at this I have drawn on material held by the British Film Institute's Reuben Library, whose holdings include issues of *Sleazoid*

Express, European Trash Cinema, Ungawa! and the British fanzine, *Shock Xpress*. I have also made use of online blogs and sites which have served as archives in their own way: Post Modern Trashology (www.postmodern-trashaeology.thezombified.com), moviemags.com, the European Trash Cinema forum (europeantrashcinema.blogspot.co.uk/p/forum.html.) and the Pulp Magazine Archive at the Internet Archive (www.archive.org) as well as secondary sources such as Sanjek's article and Antonio Lázaro-Rebell's more recent discussion of *European Trash Cinema* (2016). Having focused up till now on the United States, and to some extent on New York, this chapter starts out from the same location but also considers trash cinema as an international phenomenon, if partly through its American reception. The focus here is on the late twentieth century cult of trash rather than the films themselves, but in the final part of this chapter I look at more contemporary examples of that cult in terms of the celebration of the bad and the trashy, through the appropriation of material produced for quite different purposes (in the form of the 'Christian Scare Film') but also material that is deliberately produced with an eye on its potential cult appeal.

From Sleazoid to Shock

Sleazoid Express has come to be known through the 2002 book written by Landis and Clifford. As Austin Fisher and Johnny Walker note, the book has served as a 'chronicle and myth-generator' (2016: 4) in its tour through different New York grindhouse cinemas and the sub-genres in which they specialised. However the zine began as a listing of screenings and other events, reporting on a narrow location, with its own particular stance but not initially entirely restricted to the grindhouse cinema or the exploitation genre. Following on from the 'art and trash' emphasis of the second issue, issue three highlighted a Sam Fuller retrospective at the Museum of Modern Art and Stan Brakhage's *Dog Star Man* (1964) at the Anthology Archives, alongside reports on *Driller Killer* (1979) ('the germ of a good idea, but it emerged as one of the most irritating ripoffs I've encountered in the past year') and a note about the forthcoming 'The Hostage [*Held Hostage*, 1977] which looks as if it might be a nasty little exploitation item'. Coming attractions in the following issue included both Russ Meyer's *Vixen!* (1968) and Kenneth Anger's *Invocation of My Demon*

Brother (1969), while the forthcoming presentations listed in issue five include *Chelsea Girls* (with Ondine as guest speaker) as well as *Caged Heat* (1974), *The Big Doll House* (1971) and *Private Parts* (1972).

To an extent this connects *Sleazoid Express* to a longer tradition going back to Mekas's 1960s viewing habits and the highbrow appeal of the Rialto in the 1930s. Looking forward, Landis's juxtaposition of European exploitation next to the American avant-garde suggests a comparison with what Joan Hawkins identified in mail order catalogues that listed classics of European art cinema next to American exploitation films, challenging assumptions about the presumed opposition of prestige and popular culture and revealing the extent to which high and low culture trade in the same images, tropes and themes (1999: 15). However, such relations brought their own tensions. Landis himself later reported that while Kenneth Anger loved *Sleazoid Express*, Mekas and Ken Jacobs hated it (2002: xiv). From the other side, the first issue of *Gore Gazette* began with a complaint about Landis 'hanging around with Andrew Sarris, Jonas Mekas or others from that dreaded circle of "lobster" critics' and about his increasingly critical and analytical approach to 'films that just don't hold up to that style of criticism and were never made to...'. One trend was to move away from any artistic, avant-garde or critical pretensions, or from any suggestion of sexual diversity. While the films of Jack Smith, George and Mike Kuchar and John Waters had used trash to challenge sexual norms, the new cult of exploitation trash was often insistent in asserting its masculinity and its freedom to offend. Its shock tactics ranged from graphic cover imagery to the 'Joe Bob Briggs' redneck persona adopted by John Bloom for his *Dallas Times Herald* drive-in movie column.

The British fanzine *Shock Xpress*, first published in 1985, provides a different example, indicating the evolving nature of this form of cinephilia. It emphasised informed comment on exploitation cinema while covering a territory that ranged from Chunk Norris to George Kuchar, though it prefaced the latter with the apology that 'it's not often that *Shock Xpress* sings the praises of gay 'underground' film makers, so allow this reviewer his one indulgence' (Sim 1988–89: 36). At the other end of the spectrum, attention to a major release could provoke reader criticism: 'I don't think coverage of mainstream material like *The Bride* [1985] is what your magazine should be looking towards,' complained one reader. '*Tonight I will eat your Corpse* [1967] in the same issue is *Shock Xpress* on the nose!'

(Kerekes 1986: 6). In Britain the approach to this subject matter was coloured by the Video Recordings Act of 1984, with its ban on videos deemed to be unsuitable for home viewing. Thus 'trash' was defined not just on the grounds of taste or the distinctions employed by the film industry, or in terms of the legitimate and the illegitimate, but also as legal and illegal categories. As Kate Egan has documented, this outlaw status was another way that for particular audiences trash could be converted into treasure. Titles identified as 'video nasties' became subcultural capital, while after the easing of regulations a 'previously banned' sticker could be used as a promotional device and the work of directors such as Hershell Gordon Lewis and Jesus Franco could be reframed within the quality press on the basis that 'their films' initial status as notorious "trash" has blocked a British cultural appreciation of the films' refreshing bad taste and ironic black humour' (2007: 249).

The Psychotronic

Trash was not understood only in terms of exploitation cinema. The 'psychotronic' as defined in the zine published by Michael Weldon from 1980 and the subsequent publications that used the psychotronic name was a more eclectic category, in line with the status that Sconce gave *The Psychotronic Encyclopedia of Film* as the most visible document of the paracinema community (1995: 372). *Psychotronic* looked back to hosted television horror shows such as *Shock Theater* as well as to a broader range of old films broadcast on American television. '*Psychotronic* films range from sincere social commentary to degrading trash,' wrote Weldon in the introduction of *The Psychotronic Encyclopedia of Film* (1989: xii). This suggests it was not limited to trash but adopted an open policy that included trash, seemingly along with everything else. Covering titles from *Abbot and Costello Go to Mars* (1953) to *Zotz!* (1962), *The Psychotronic Encyclopedia of Film* emphasised exploitation and oddities but found space for blockbusters such as *Jaws* (1975) and older classics. *Ninotchka* (1939) has an entry, on the basis that the cast includes psychotronic star Bela Lugosi. While this is clearly not helpful for any attempt to pin the term down, it highlights the underlying principle of inclusiveness. While cult audiences have often been seen in terms of exclusivity, one side to the cult of trash was the principle that nothing was to be discarded.

The *Psychotronic Encylopedia of Film* was also characterised by an emphasis on recovery rather than commentary. It lists the forgotten, often with no more than a brief synopsis: in *Louisiana Hussy* (1960), 'Dangerous Cajun beauty ruins every life she touches, breaking up families and eventually causing the suicide of a young bride' (1983: 433), while *Love Me Deadly* (1972) is 'A psychological horror film about a woman (Mary Wilcox) who loves corpses and a homosexual mortuary-attendant killer' (1983: 434). Some entries combine plot details with brief judgments: *Love Butcher* (1975) is 'An extremely ridiculous psycho movie about Caleb, a balding, crippled gardener constantly mistreated by his female sub-urban Los Angeles employees... Despite the title, the film is very tame by today's standards' (ibid.). The overall tone is one of neutrality varied by flashes of enthusiasm or dismissal. The quarterly magazine version was different. The much clearer allegiance to the paracinema community of *Psychotronic Video* is evident in the advertisements from video sup-pliers such as Something Weird, Video Wasteland, Tapes of Terror and Scorched Earth Productions, alongside news of other fanzines and fea-tures devoted to all forms of the psychotronic, from classic Hollywood to softcore pornography.

Incredibly Strange Films

A different, but shifting and related picture is evident in Jim Morton's *Trashola* and *Incredibly Strange Films*. *Trashola* began as a free 'Schlock and Horror Newsletter', with an emphasis on horror, though with reviews of relatively mainstream films as well as the low budget and the obscure. The eighth issue begins with a review of the John Waters' film, *Polyester* (1981), alongside briefer comments on *Demonoid* (1981) and *Looker* (1981); the same issue includes reviews of Paul Schrader's *Cat People* (1982), *Blade Runner* (1982) and *Jaws III* (1983). The mainstream was included alongside the marginal. By issue thirteen *Trashola* had become 'The newsletter for the fan of the grotesque'.

Morton's *Incredibly Strange Films* contributions consisted of entries on Russ Meyer, David Friedman, Biker films, J.D. (juvenile delinquent) films, beach party films, LSD films, women in prison films, the Mexican horror star Santo, sexploitation films, educational films, *Daughter of Horror* (1953), *Spider Baby* (1968), Edward D. Wood Jr. and an A-Z of personalities from Al Adamson to Albert Zugsmith. Developing Weldon's eclectic approach, this was a devotion to cultural detritus from *Trapped by Mormons* (1922) to *Good Grooming for Girls* (1956). In this account, the Highway Safety Film *Signal 30* (1959) shown across American high schools (and in 2012 used as the title for the fifth episode of the fifth season of *Mad Men*) becomes an unintentional 'gore classic' for its graphic depiction of car crash injuries and it is noted that 'some of the best filmmakers around' from Frank Capra to Russ Meyer have made educational and industrial films (Morton 1986: 166–7).

Morton's extension of auteur theory was evident at *Trashola*. In the sixteenth issue, his discussion of *It! The Terror from Beyond Space* (1958) identified Edward L. Cahn, the film's otherwise unappreciated director, as one of several 'whose only crime was their ability to work under the strictures of studio budgets, crews, writers and schedules'. Later (Vol. 3 No. 1), he promised to make up for the fact that, 'Like most film critics I have been guilty of avoiding the hardcore porno films ... it seems a bit unfair of me to ignore what may well be the last bastion of the independent hack filmmaker'. An auteurist approach to trash cinema was also central to the introduction to *Incredibly Strange Films*. In what was in effect a paracinematic manifesto, V. Vale and Andrea Juno made the case for 'low-class' and 'low-brow' films as 'sources of pure enjoyment and delight', which had been filtered and blocked by middle-class values and the dictatorship of 'good taste' (1986: 4). While Hollywood was inhibited by the corporate chain of command, low-budget filmmaking allowed films to be 'transcendent expressions of a single person's individual vision and quirky originality' (1986: 5). The films of directors such as Hershell Gordon Lewis and Dennis Steckler (whose *Incredibly Strange Creatures Who Stopped Living and Became Mixed-Up Zombies* [1964] gave Vale and Juno their title) were thus worthwhile on three grounds:

> First of all: unfettered creativity. Often the films are eccentric – even *extreme* – presentations by individuals *freely expressing their imaginations*, who throughout the filmmaking process improvise creative solutions to problems posed either by circumstance or budget – mostly the latter. Secondly, they often present unpopular – even radical – views addressing social, political, racial or sexual inequalities, hypocrisy in religion or government; or in other ways

they assault taboos related to the presentation of sexuality, violence and other mores. (Cf. George Romero's *Dead* trilogy which features intelligent, problem-solving black heroes, or Russ Meyer's *Faster, Pussycat! Kill! Kill!* which showcases tough girls outwitting – and even physically outdoing – sexist men.) Thirdly, occasionally films are made of such unique stature (Cf. *Daughter of Horror*) as to stand virtually outside any genre or classification, thus extending the boundaries of what has been done in the medium, as well as pro- viding – at best – inexplicably marvellous experiences. (1986: 5–6)

Sconce has claimed that this rhetoric 'could just as easily be at home in an elite discussion of the French New Wave or the American New Cinema' (1995: 382). It also led Jancovich to note the absurdity of appealing to the freedom from commercial and ideological demands of films that were defined in terms of commerce or education, and to point to the tension evi- dent in Morton's description of the cross-cutting in *Plan 9 from Outer Space* as 'bordering on Dada', or comparing the 'grossness' of *Daughter of Horror* with that of the French arthouse film, *Le Grande Bouffe* (1973) (2002: 314). *Incredibly Strange Films* was presented as a challenge to legitimate culture but this was often undertaken through appeal to high cultural values.

   Such a tension is not unique to this form of cinephilia. From the begin- ning notions of film authorship had been driven by an appeal of the low and to the high. Sarris's 'Notes on the Auteur Theory in 1962' begins with a quote from Søren Kierkegaard before before citing Tolstoy, Shakespeare and Mozart among others. The subsequent cult of trash cinema also fed off a more general pop surrealism in its references to Dada and the 'inex- plicably marvellous'. The surrealist interest in low-brow cinema has long been acknowledged but its relationship to popular culture also involved the popularisation of surrealist ideas and images. Thus *Incredibly Strange Films* latched on to the surrealist notion of the marvellous as beauty achieved through a shock to the system and an escape from cultural norms and conventions.

European Trash

The pursuit of the incredibly strange was accompanied by what could be a more traditional but nuanced and contextualised concern with trash cinema, facilitated by changes in how films were consumed. Publications such as *Trashola* and *Incredibly Strange Films* were part of a broader move to extend the range of films seen as worthy of serious attention. They appeared in an environment in which the means through which films were consumed was changing, and in which there was a new interest in the popular dimension of international cinema. Since 1980, Landis had documented how the cinemas around Times Square had come to rely on genre films from Europe, Asia and Latin America. However, this form of global exploitation cinema was restricted to major metropolitan centres and diminishing in its scale. The increasing availability of films on video was central to the expanding interest in the obscure, offbeat and (in particular) Italian. According to Raiford Guins, 'Prior to videocassette and its largescale "home penetration" in the mid-1980s, Italian horror "films" (when distributed and shown on U.S. screens) were exhibited in limited release, or found on the midnight movie circuit, or at paracinema festivals, or at drive-in cinemas after their post-War glamour period had run its course' (2005: 16). Nationwide exhibition was only made possible by the VCR, and subsequently by other video or, more recently, web-based formats.

It was this changing environment that Craig Ledbetter responded to, first through *Hi-Tech Terror*, then *European Trash Cinema*. In its initial issues, *Hi-Tech Terror*'s lists of new releases and box-office hits accompanied more general video and satellite news and reviews, with the emphasis on the more obscure titles as well as tape transfer quality. This technical concern runs through the early issues, in which Ledbetter (initially the sole contributor) discussed issues such as different tape formats (a concern pursued more extensively in Tim Lucas's *Video Watchdog: The Perfectionist Guide to Fantastic Video*) and Hollywood's opposition to the VCR. The initial reports mention films such as *Nightmare on Elm Street* (1984) and *Friday the 13th: The Final Chapter* (1984), and the reviews include American re-releases such as *She Freak*, the 1967 version of *Freaks* (for Ledbetter 'one of the worst films I have seen for some time'). However, Ledbetter's diminishing interest in American cinema became increasingly evident. In issue 33 it led to the following statement:

> I don't give a shit A) What Larry Cohen is doing, B) How Sam Raimi
> plans on remaking *Evil Dead* for the rest of his life, or C) The fact

there are hundreds of straight-to-video American made Junk waiting to find a home in someone's VCR. *I JUST DON'T CARE...* We
Americans refuse to recognise the tremendous amount of super-
lative work taking place overseas. We'd rather fawn over Tobe
Hooper Abortions from Cannon (next up is *Empire*), thank Charles
Band for resurrecting the drive-in double-bill so we can see two
turds for the price of one and interview Hershell Gordon Lewis
for the 50th time. C'mon folks, show some originality. (Quoted in
Sanjek 2000: 316)

Ledbetter's diatribe had an effect beyond the 250 subscribers of *Hi-Tech
Terror* (see Lázaro-Reboll 2016: 34). It in part fits the pattern of competing
fans 'trashing' the mainstream and other trash fans in the way in which
it dismisses the contemporary American horror and splatter film. It was
followed most immediately by *European Trash Cinema*, which Ledbetter
established in 1988, announced as 'devoted entirely to European genre
films ... I guarantee that this journal has no interest in U.S. films and there
will be no coverage of it in ETC'.

In the editorial for the seventh issue (quoted by Lázaro-Reboll 2016:
36) Ledbetter hailed 1989 as:

a very good year for Euro-Trash lovers [since] we saw the debut of
many fine film publications that catered to our particular obsessions (most came from Great Britain as usual), plus the stalwarts
SPAGETTI CINEMA & WESTERNS ALL'ITALIANA here in the US continued to appear...

Ledbetter's use of the term 'trash', more specifically 'Euro-trash', is a further sign of the term's shifting connotations. As noted earlier, his irony
was directed at critics rather than at the films. Ledbetter and other contributors to the zine identified as connoisseurs rather than ironists. The
focus of the zine was on the Italian horror film and the giallo, but it also
covered other examples of European genre cinema. It went beyond this in
referring to films such as the Argentinian *Blood of the Virgins* (1967) and
the Mexican *She-Wolf* (1965), stretching the meaning of 'European', as
Lázaro-Reboll notes, while confirming the overall concern with bringing
foreign horror to the attention and view of American audiences (2016: 37).

That is, zines such as *European Trash Cinema* functioned to review and evaluate films and discuss them but also as part of a network, tracking down obscure and rare films and bringing them to the attention of like-minded individuals. Their quest was for the good rather than the bad.

In providing an alternative strand of film criticism, *European Trash Cinema* looked at films awaiting academic legitimisation but without appealing to paracinematic reading strategies. As Lázaro-Reboll puts it, through their particular generic focus, reviewers 'held on to traditional viewing pleasures like understanding films, directors and subgenres in relation to each other and to other related media which shared a common ground' (2016: 47). European trash (but also other non-American versions) was identified as having an appeal because it offered qualities lacking in contemporary American cinema, and also because of its rarity. According to one editorial (Vol. 2 No. 2), 'a lot of fans are getting real bored with the U.S. film scene. After you have seen all the sequels, the shot-on-video atrocities, the big budget sleaze you realise everyone is stuck in neutral. So you start looking elsewhere, overseas for instance, for something different.' This strand of European cinema could offer an alternative to the arthouse, allowing *European Trash Cinema* to include a feature by Ric Menello on 'The Trashy Art of Claude Chabrol' (2.8, 30–5) but in the main to concentrate on filmmakers working exclusively within genre conventions.

The trans-Atlantic dimension to trash cinema existed as a European interest in American culture as well as the other way round. The Spanish *2000maniacos* announced its American concern in its title, derived from Hershell Gordon Lewis's *Two Thousand Maniacs!* (1964), and initial cover, featuring Tod Browning's *Freaks* (1932), but went on to devote itself to disreputable Spanish and European cinema more generally alongside American exploitation and pornography. These different zines existed as part of an international network. A 1989 review of fanzines in the British *Sheer Filth* (no.8) listed *Eyeball: The European Sex & Horror Review*, *Necronomicon x Mortis* ('the editors like Troma and trash') and *Ungawa!* from Britain, the Canadian *Killbaby,* the Polish *Antytabu*, and *Killer Kung Fu Enema Nurses on Crack* from New Zealand as well as the American *City Morgue.*

This international trash culture varied in content and presentation. Published in 1990, the second issue of the British *Ungawa!* mixed

American pulp culture, from Betty Page to the 'hardboiled' crime novels of Frederic Brown, with a fascination with continental genre cinema, including 'An Introduction to Spanish Horror'. The film reviews include *College Girls Confidential* (1966) ('good clean, unmissable smut') and the nudie cutie *Kiss Me Quick* (1964) but also non-American films such as *Hercules Against the Moonmen* (1964) ('The whole plot is ludicrous, improbable and full of holes, but who cares – it's Peplum') and a compilation tape titled *Drive-In Sleaze* that nonetheless included 'some great gonzoid Euro pap including *The Reluctant Sadist* [Denmark, 1967] and an incredible trailer for [the German] *The Tower of Screaming Virgins*'. In this instance, Europe is seen to offer something lacking in what Francois Choquet in the Spanish horror introduction described as 'the staid, stuffy and stiff films churned out in Britain'. Their preoccupations 'were usually more unrestrained, they squelched around in areas that bordered on the tasteless and the taboo. More importantly the plot ideas were also stranger, more unusual and crazily outlandish.'

We can get an idea of the approach adopted in *Ungawa!* through its review of the Italian film, *Bloody Pit of Horror* (1965). The film begins with a supposed quote from the Marquis de Sade ('My vengeance needs blood') and a sixteenth-century scene featuring the Crimson Executioner. It stars Mickey Hargitay as the body-building and narcissistic Travis Anderson, whose isolation is interrupted by a film crew hoping to use his castle as a setting for their latest giallo. The visitors are then killed or tortured with varying degrees of elaboration by a figure dressed as the Crimson Executioner. On page 14 *Ungawa!* urged its readers to

Forget those arseholes the critics and give this sucker a chance. After all it's got some of the stuff we know and love: obsession, perversion and distorted psychosis. But before you cream yourself be prepared for patches of cocktail type musak and high camp mixed in with the menace and diabolical torture. It's a film which veers between the serious and the schmaltzy. Yet thank God for it, and all those other Euro-Horrors soaked in the erotic and the macabre, at least they tackled areas where other filmmakers feared to tread... *Bloody Pit* is no masterpiece but who really cares? It has its moments of madness, delirium and daftness, sometimes that's more than enough for any film.

The opposition here is clear: on the one side the critics and the values of the quality film, on the other side Euro-horrors soaked in the erotic and the macabre: obsession, perversion and distorted psychosis. In between exists the more ambivalent territory of cocktail-type musak and high camp.

Publications such as *Ungawa!* and *European Trash Cinema*, as well as books such as *Immoral Tales*, were important for directing attention to films and filmmakers overlooked elsewhere as well as for their more general stance. They have been followed by more academic publications such as *Alternative Europe: Eurotrash and Exploitation Cinema Since 1945*. In the introduction to this, Ernest Mathijs and Xavier Mendix explicitly set their work against the 'high white tradition', and against the tendency to ignore 'nasty and trashy European cinema' (2004: 3). It is a sign of a shift within film studies that the contributions to the book include Leon Hunt discussing *Bloody Pit of Horror*. Far from dismissing the film, for Hunt *Bloody Pit of Horror* is worthy of study, significant in relation to Italian economic growth in the 1950s and 1960s, the hybridity of the *peplum* and the *giallo*, and the fantasies Sigmund Freud explored in his essay 'A Child is Being Beaten'. In dressing up as the Crimson Executioner, Travis is performing a role libidinous and puritanical, in a sadomasochistic homosexual phantasy.

Hunt's analysis rejects an auteurist approach: the film's director, Massimo Pupillo, lacks a recognisable signature. Yet he begins with the observation that what reputation the film has is 'largely confined to the ambivalent psychotronic gaze of trash aesthetics' (2004: 173). While it lacks a recognised auteur, Hunt notes that what it does have is an extraordinary barnstorming performance by former Mr Universe Mickey Hargitay:

> it is worth pondering the relationship between bodybuilding, sadistic spectacle and male narcissism. To do so, however, we need to put trash aesthetics on one side for a moment and think about cultural and generic context. Put simply, however deliriously out-of-this-world trash 'classics' may seem, they *do* come from somewhere. (2004: 174)

By 'psychotronic gaze', Hunt has in mind comments such as 'sick piece of sixties schlock' (L. Balbo in *Shock: The Essential Guide to Exploitation Cinema*), 'a great sleaze-trash classic' (Amazon customer review) and 'a breathtaking blend of cheesecake, pop art and Sadean excess' (Frank Heinen-lotter's liner notes for the *Something Weird* DVD) (2004: 173). Accounts that attempt to measure its cinematic achievement were less enthusiastic. He notes, for instance, that 'Cathal Tohill and Pete Tombs clearly like it, but find it "too daft to be described as bona fide sadism"' (ibid.).

The case here is that the psychotronic gaze of trash aesthetics removes the film from its context and from a critical perspective. Complicating this are the variations within those aesthetics. In referring to Tohill and Tombs' reservations about the film, Hunt was citing their book, *Immoral Tales*, which in fact largely reproduced the *Ungawa!* review of *Bloody Pit of Horror*, with a slight modification of enthusiasm so that 'no masterpiece but really cares?' became 'an uneven film, one that veers from comic strip dementia to inconsequential noodling and back again' (1994: 38). *The Psychotronic Encyclopedia of Film* itself dismissed the film as 'A classic of silly sadism and bad acting' (1989: 77). In other instances, those with a taste for trash could be more critical or, in the words of Lázaro-Reboll, produce writing 'characterised by a distinctive style attentive to the films' circulation as part of wider industrial and cultural trends and sensitive to the generic bloodlines flowing through them' (2016: 46). On the other hand, more academic accounts that place trash cinema in its industrial and cultural context have not neglected the delirious. Thus, Hunter opens his detailed and scholarly study, *British Trash Cinema*, with a discussion of *Slave Girls* (1967) as 'what trash cinema itself is all about – those precious fleeting moments when the commercial stumbles haphazardly into the erotically oneiric and avant-garde' (2013: vi). He goes on to describe 'this innocently hapless film' as 'perfect for obsession and flights of writerly fantasy – or is that just special pleading by an over-excited "trash aesthete" hot for the thrills of weirdness and obscurity?' The broader picture here is thus one in which film studies as an academic discipline now includes trash and the psychotronic, the films and the sensibility, just as in their own way fan publications ranged from the pursuit of moments of madness to more nuanced appreciation and evaluation.

The Bad Film in the 21st Century

Along with other zines, *European Trash Cinema* continued online, as both a mail order service and (at least between 2014 and 2016) a forum, containing film reviews as well as uploads of early issues of *Hi-Tech Terror* and other zines. It represents one strand of criticism that has used the label of 'trash' while holding on to traditional viewing pleasures. It contrasts with other forms of cult celebration of the bad, evident in 'Bad Film' clubs, one-off screenings of films such as *The Room*, *Troll 2* (2007) parties, themed websites, Facebook pages, video reviews and discussions and lists of worst films. In a report on 'The Bad Film Society' in Ashland, Oregon, founder Ed Polish explained that most people who attended were 'culturally astute. ... They may be the same people who attend the Oregon Shakespeare Festival. They like the best 1 percent of good and bad culture. They just don't like the 98 percent in the middle. ... Bad movies are unintentionally funny and entertaining, and we encourage people to provide commentary in the manner of *Mystery Science Theater 3000*' (Anon. 2012). Films screened include *Shakes the Clown* (2009), *Island of Lost Souls* (1932), *Cobra Woman* (1944), *The Swinger* (1966), *The Garbage Pail Kids Movie* (1987), *A Bucket of Blood* (1960), *Troll 2* and *If Footmen Tire You, What Will Horses Do?* (1971).

This at least indicates that 'bad' is, like paracinema, an elastic concept. Three of the above films get an entry in *The Psychotronic Encylopedia of Film*. *Island of Lost Souls* is described as 'probably the best horror film ever made' (Weldon 1989: 376), Corman's intentionally funny *A Bucket of Blood* is 'an all-time classic' (1989: 93), while the Maria Montez film, *Cobra Woman*, is 'extraordinary', 'kitsch' and 'outrageous' (1989: 123). Celebrated by Jack Smith and on the cover of the British edition of *Incredibly Strange Films*, Montez and *Cobra Woman* have acquired iconic status within this field. In their different ways, both *The Garbage Pail Kids Movie* and *Troll 2* are widely accepted as 'bad films', and the latter in particular developed a strong cult following on that basis (see Ian Olney's discussion of its passage from forgettable Italian horror to cyberspace and midnight movie sensation; 2013: 70–82). Bobcat Goldthwait's black comedy *Shakes the Clown* owes its cult reputation to the *Boston Globe*'s Betsy Sherman once describing it as the '*Citizen Kane* of alcoholic clown movies' (2009). Directed by Hollywood veteran George Sidney and starring Ann-Margaret, *The Swinger* rates an entry in *Bad Movies We Love*, where Edward Margulies and Stephen Rebello claim that it 'just might be the all-time tackiest major studio movie' (1983: 242).

If Footmen Tire You, What Will Horses Do? is a rather different example that bears further examination. As a 'Christian Scare Film' (one of the weird categories listed on the 'Something Weird' website) it can be linked to the educational films celebrated in *Incredibly Strange Films*, in particular to those films appropriated as 'gore classics' for their use of horror imagery in order to convey their message. As a film directed by Ron Ormond, who had earlier directed films such as *Mesa of Lost Women* (1953) and *The Monster and the Stripper* (1968), it owes its approach to low-budget and exploitation cinema. It is distinctive in how far it takes that and in the way it is used to illustrate a hell-fire sermon.

If Footmen Tire You... was the first of three collaborations between Ormond and preacher Estus Pirkle, the others being *The Burning Hell* (1974) and *The Believers' Heaven* (1977). Wanting to make a film version of his hellfire sermon, 'If Footmen Tire You, What Will Horses Do?' the Rev. Pirkle turned to Ormond, notwithstanding the lurid nature of the filmmaker's previous work. Ormond agreed, having apparently found a new religious commitment following a recent near-death experience. The result was a tract warning of the dangers of the imminent Communist invasion ('I can document every statement I make in this film', announces Pirkle at the beginning) and the need for religious salvation. In the film, Pirkle's sermon persuades a young woman to realise the error of her ways, while for the film audience his warnings are dramatised by scenes showing what the godless Cuban Communists will do when Christian indolence has allowed them to overrun the country. This ranges from seven-day working weeks, from five in the morning till nine at night, to brainwashing, torture and mass slaughter, illustrated with bodies strewn across the ground, splattered with red paint. Violence against children is emphasised, most notoriously in one scene in which a boy is prevented from hearing the voice of God by having bamboo shoots pushed into his ears: the insertion into the ears is not seen, but the boy's vomiting is.

In his discussion of 'abject horror' as a form of 'trash horror', Hunter distinguishes between those films appreciated as failed horror and those where the badness is equally defined by grossness. Generally dated back to Hershell Gordon Lewis's *Blood Feast*, the gore film has been a calculated exercise in bad taste, the offensive and disgusting. As such, they are less easily re-evaluated as 'good' than even a film made by *Cannibal Holocaust* director, Ruggero Deodato. In asking how we can understand the appeal of such films, I. Q. Hunter speculated that they could offer a paradoxical comfort blanket, positing a cultist return to the abject as 'a way, both masterful and masochistic, of coping with threatening images and experiences and domesticating them through compulsive repetition' (2014: 497–8). *If Footmen Tire You...* was made to take away that blanket. Rather than box-office takings, it sets out to save souls, and apparently has been highly successful as a hellfire sermon, though not to the extent of its successor, *The Burning Hell* (see Ridley 2010: 232). In the words of Jim Ridley, it is an example of how 'Christian exploitation' adopts 'the look and content of trash only as a means of furthering its messianic aims' (2010: 229).

These aims are complicated by the dual authorship of the sermonising Pirkle and Ormond's near Hershell Gordon Lewis-style approach to violence. The film is both hellfire sermon and hixsploitation horror. It has lent itself to appropriation that contradicts its preferred meaning, as when the film's soundtrack, of loudspeakers repeating 'Christianity is stupid' as an example of Communist brainwashing, was sampled by Negativland. Its cartoon Communists invite laughter. It remains a disturbing and disturbed film.

If Footmen Tire You... is 'cinema from the cultural margins' but in its own particular way. A broader sense of the contemporary trash audience was provided by the online survey undertaken in Germany in 2014 by Keyvan Sarkhosh and Winfried Menninghaus with a view to acquiring empirical data on audiences identifying themselves as viewers of trash films. Their sample identified amusement as the main response to trash films, an amusement 'mostly associated with an *ironic viewing stance* and, to a lesser degree, *trangression*' (2016: 9). Trash was linked to cheapness and appeared to overlap with the concept of the exploitation film but with limitations: it was associated with the horror film rather than sexploitation. In line with the argument of Sconce and others, trash films were commonly identified as 'anti-establishment' films', and their main appeal appeared to be to a male, highly educated audience (2016: 13). It was this last conclusion that was picked up in the press, leading to a spate of newspaper headlines on the links between high intelligence and trash (see, for instance, Hooton 2016).

Sharknado (2013), the film mentioned the most by those taking part in the survey, is a cult film in a different way to the other film mentioned in this chapter. Its story of a hurricane that causes sharks to descend on, and swim through, Los Angeles, and the steps taken to fight back against this menace, is consciously absurd. When shown on the Syfy Channel on 11 July 2013 it attracted unspectacular viewing figures (1.37 million) but a higher number of comments on Twitter, at one point peaking at around 5,000 tweets a minute (see Stelter 2013: C3). Syfy Channel repeats attracted larger audiences and it was given a limited cinema release. It has (at the time of writing) been followed by *Sharknado 2: The Second One* (which attracted a larger audience when aired in 2014 on Syfy and was again given a cinema release), *Sharknado: The Video Game* (2014), *How To Survive a Sharknado and Other Disasters* (published by Three Rivers Press in 2014), *Sharknado 3: Oh Hell No!* (2015), *Sharknado: The 4th Awakens* (2016) and *Sharknado 5... Earth 0* (2017). Thus one strand of twenty-first-century trash cinema came as pre-packaged cult entertainment.

Such films, sometimes given a limited cinema release but made for television or video, also serve as contemporary B-films. Syfy had commissioned *Sharknado* from Asylum, a company best known for producing 'mockbusters' such as *The Da Vinci Treasure* (2006), *Snakes on a Train* (2006) and *Atlantic Rim* (2013): films released around the same time as their near namesakes in an attempt to benefit from their higher profile. Asylum moved to this strategy from their earlier, straight-to-horror-video approach when their *War of the Worlds* (2005), apparently coincidentally released around the same time as the Spielberg film of the same name, proved a seller at Blockbusters. Subsequently developed into a deliberate strategy, according to Rolf Potts this new form of B movie was aimed at three kinds of viewer: those who 'have seen the real blockbuster and want more of the same thing, no matter how lo-fi', the 'genre geeks, interested in low-budget adventure and sci-fi films', and those renting the movie thinking it is something else, who may end up complaining on the web that they have been duped (2007: E18). IMDb User Reviews for Asylum films include 'i [sic] got this trash for free and I WANT MY MONEY BACK!', (jmajors3, 2007, on *Transmorphers* [2007]) and 'I was expecting to see a funny trash [sic], but I found an awfully boring movie, with no story, dreadful acting and cheap CGi [sic]' (Carvalho 2014, on *Abraham Lincoln vs. Zombies* [2012]).

The Asylum films in general and the *Sharknado* franchise in particular exist within a broader context: Troma films from *Splatter University* (1984) to *Poultrygeist: Night of the Chicken Dead* (2006), earlier deliberate trash such as *Attack of the Killer Tomatoes* (1977) and *Killer Klowns from*

Outer Space (1988), and a host of other films that play up their absurdity whether as out-and-out parody or in the *Sharktopus vs. Pteracuda* (2014) action-film mode. Thus the contemporary 'bad film' operates between different poles. At one end of the scale it is industry driven, a calculated attempt to appeal to a particular market, accentuating absurdities in a way that is played straight but designed for laughter. At the other end of the scale it is a deliberate misreading, dependent on the failure of a film's aspiration and working to transform it into something else.

Conclusion

The cult of trash is not new but it gained a particular impetus in the final decades of the twentieth century. This took place at a time of change in how films were consumed, as existing forms of cinema exhibition contracted (over time) while the growth of video and later the internet led to a new market and to new networks of exchange and debate. It was driven also by a post-punk self-publishing culture and a new generation asserting their own tastes and distastes. It varied in different national and cultural contexts, with different regimes of censorship leading to different levels of access and to variations in what acquired rarity value in this subcultural exchange. If that landscape as a whole has changed, leading to a more global cult and culture, and to numerous previously obscure films becoming easier to access, this has also been accompanied by more local events, in which trash is celebrated through audience participation and performance.

These different viewing contexts make it difficult to sustain large claims for a devotion to trash cinema as an oppositional practice. Paracinema could be political but ironic readings have taken different forms while a self-declared interest in trash can invoke irony at the expense of critical hierarchies as well as through film-viewing position. Trash has meant good as well as bad but has also existed as a category containing its own highs and lows. Ironic consumption has been adopted as an oppositional stance but also as a form of entertainment.

What this does not do is establish a set of essential characteristics of trash cinema. The end of the twentieth century and the beginning of the twenty-first has been a period when trash cinema has emerged as more than a term of disparagement, though complaints about 'this trash' can still be found in IMDb reviews and elsewhere. The form that the reclamation of trash has taken has varied from an appeal to high cultural values to a fascination with trash as trash and an enjoyment of 'funny trash'. The films cited here have not been discussed as exemplary instances of trash cinema and have often moved in and out of that area depending on context even if the cult of trash involves viewing a film out of context, as inexplicably marvellous.

5   FROM FLASH GORDON TO BAYTEKIN

Everybody wanted to be Flash. Not Eddie. Eddie had no competi-
tion ... he wanted to be Dale! (John Andrews, quoted in Grey 1995:
16)

John Andrews' anecdote about Edward D. Wood Jr.'s childhood highlights
what is (relatively) common knowledge, about Wood's transvestism, the
popularity of the *Flash Gordon* serials in the 1930s, and that audiences
respond in different ways and can be, literally or metaphorically, transvestite. Building on this, in this final chapter I focus on film versions of
Flash Gordon as a way of providing an overview of the changing forms
of trash cinema, in terms of audiences and reception but also the texts
themselves. Universal's *Flash Gordon* serials achieved a remarkably high
profile on their first release but remained associated with the low cinema
form of the film serial. The serials continued to circulate for decades after
their first screenings, at children's matinees, at midnight screenings, on
television ... and the character remained a name to be checked on the
basis of a combination of high profile and low cultural status. That status
took a different and lower form in 1974 with the release of the softcore
Flesh Gordon, and experienced a further dip again in 1990 with *Flesh
Gordon Meets the Cosmic Cheerleaders*. The release of a big-budget,
feature version in 1980, to a mixed reception, complicates the picture,
as does that film's camp and developing cult status. A further complica-

tion comes in the shape of *Baytekin Fezada Çarpışanlar*, also known as *Flash Gordon: Battle in Space*, a Turkish variant initially released in 1967 and subsequently revived on YouTube and other internet sites, where it is often listed under the 'psychotronic' tag. The discussion here does not extend to the German *Flash Gordon* series broadcast in 1954 and 1955, Sci-Fi Channel's *Flash Gordon* (2007–8) or (disappointingly) to *Sesame Street*'s 'The Adventures of Trash Gordon'. However, looking at different film versions and variations can draw out the heterogeneous nature of trash cinema, and how it has shifted across the decades.

The Universal Serials

Flash Gordon was never obscure trash. The character had a high-profile existence from his first appearance as an Alex Raymond comic strip on 7 January 1934. The stories were quickly adapted, first for radio, then cinema, with Buster Crabbe as Flash Gordon in Universal's *Flash Gordon* (1936), *Flash Gordon's Trip to Mars* (1938) and *Flash Gordon Conquers the Universe* (1940). Buster Crabbe also starred in a further Universal science fiction serial, *Buck Rogers* (1939). The *Flash Gordon* serials were in turn released in different feature versions. The first serial became *Rocket Ship*. To cash in on the success of Orson Welles' *War of the Worlds* broadcast, in 1938 Universal also released a feature version of *Flash Gordon's Trip to Mars*, as *Mars Attacks the World*. In 1966 the first serial was re-edited for television under the title *Spaceship to the Unknown*, while *Flash Gordon Conquers the Universe* was re-edited under the title *Purple Death from Outer Space*. All these different versions allowed Crabbe's adventures in outer space to circulate throughout the second half of the 1930s, the 1940s, and the second half of the twentieth century.

Claims that the initial film had a budget several times that of other film serials of the time and became Universal's second-biggest money-maker of the year have yet to be substantiated (see Barefoot 2017: 81–2). But the popular success and iconic importance of the serials is not in question. It was an importance quickly recognised by institutions with significant cultural capital. In autumn 1938 the British Film Institute's journal, *Sight & Sound*, put Buster Crabbe as Flash Gordon on its cover, and when the Museum of Modern Art in New York ran a season of film serials in 1942 it included an episode of Buster Crabbe's similar film serial role in *Buck Rogers*.

As a comic strip adaptation and film serial, the initial *Flash Gordon* film still remained an example of, at best, popular culture, a product not only of Hollywood but of Hollywood's lower reaches. Universal was a major studio but in the 1930s one not far from Poverty Row. It specialised in low-budget westerns, short films and serials. The film serial as a whole was held in low esteem, generally seen as a residue of an earlier phase of film history and filmmaking, appealing to children and audiences in 'neighbourhood houses' and in the often even less respected overseas market. Universal serials could rely on better than average production resources, though at the level of personnel there was some overlap with Poverty Row studios: thus Ralph Berger was art director for *Flash Gordon* and the much shoddier *The Lost City*. Universal used the studio's resources in ways that shamelessly recycled material from other films. *Flash Gordon* borrowed sets from *Bride of Frankenstein* (1935), *The Invisible Man* (1933), *The Mummy* (1932) and *Just Imagine* (1930), music from *The Invisible Man*, *The White Hell of Pitz Palu* (1929), *The Black Cat* (1934), *Bombay Mail* (1934), *Destination Unknown* (1933) and *Werewolf of London* (1935). The studio's serials were particularly reliant on stock footage, sometimes used for extended sequences. The most impressive sequences in *Flash Gordon Conquers the Universe* were the avalanche rescue scenes lifted from the German silent film, *The White Hell of Pitz-Palu* (1929), used extensively in the serial's opening two chapters.

The serials' low-production base is evident in the opening chapter of *Flash Gordon's Trip to Mars*. The first two, post-credits shots are of a pair of radio masts followed by a closely framed, minimally decorated interior shown in a single, static take. The return to Earth of Flash Gordon, Dale Arden and Dr Zarkov is largely shown through a montage of stock footage, including an extended sequence at a newspaper printers followed by assorted crowd scenes. Further stock shots are used a few minutes into the chapter, mixing diverse scenes of buildings collapsing, floods and hurricanes, with the emphasis on spectacle and action rather than narrative coherence. Performances repeatedly emphasise wide-eyed astonishment, an acting style in which Jean Rogers (as Dale Arden) excelled in particular. Exterior and cramped interior shots of the spacecraft are little more sophisticated than equivalent shots from *Plan 9 from Outer Space*. Stock music is used throughout the chapter, as was the practice across Universal serials. A simple visual iconography works through,

Fig. 13: Limited
production values
in *Flash Gordon's
Trip to Mars*

Fig. 14: Augmented
by stock footage
for scenes of
global catastrophe

for instance, identifying press reporters as either clutching cameras or scribbling on notepads. 'Humour' is introduced, but partly by showing an African-American servant who can't pronounce Mesopotamia: the lower strands of 1930s filmmaking can reveal a far more blatant racism than other Hollywood films of the time. The chapter does not display errors so much as a simplicity of narration, a simplicity that also brings the pace and dynamism characteristic of the serial.

The toning down of the imagery in the Raymond comic strips did not prevent the first *Flash Gordon* serial from the eroticisation of Dale Arden and Princess Aura. Flash Gordon himself repeatedly appeared

Fig. 15: Space travel
in *Flash Gordon's
Trip to Mars*

Fig. 16: Inside
the spacecraft
in *Plan 9 from
Outer Space*

half-naked in print drawings and the first film serial. *Flash Gordon's Trip to Mars* is less revealing. Dale dresses for space travel as if dressing for the office, a fact self-consciously alluded to in the 'I feel like a regular commuter' dialogue. In part the appeal of this, initially and subsequently, appears to have been in its image of innocence. The contemporary commentary on the serials marked them as lacking complexity and substance, but thus harmless rather than pernicious trash. Susan Sontag listed 'the old Flash Gordon comics' as a prime example of 'naïve camp' (1983: 107), but she may well have had the film serials in mind. However, as Mark Bould (2007) notes, it would be a mistake to assume that nuanced reading strategies were only available to later audiences. One of the contributors to J. P. Mayer's survey of British film tastes in the 1940s revealed divided responses in her complaints about the rowdy reception of an episode she had recently seen: 'I regard everyone who laughed at that film as a fool! They have no foresight! They have no understanding, nor did they try to understand!' (1946: 233–4). Her very insistence on the need to take seriously the film's vision of the future testifies to the existence of other responses.

In the post-war period the serials were also open to avant-garde appropriation. While Federico Fellini appears to have been more influenced by the comic strips than the films (see Bondanella 1992: 14), Kenneth Anger and Wallace Berman were fascinated by *Flash Gordon* as realised by both Alex Raymond and Buster Crabbe. Berman's Kodak Verifax collage with a Buster Crabbe/Flash Gordon still at the centre, bears the inscription, 'Portrait of Kenneth Anger'. The image also appears in Berman's film *Aleph* (1956–c.66). The suitcases displayed at 'Wanderlust', the Royal Academy's Joseph Cornell exhibition in 2015, included a *Flash Gordon* publicity still, suggesting Cornell's desire to accompany the space travellers on their trip to Mars or Mongo. Flash Gordon could be used as a symbol of an older America. David Zane Mairowitz's 1971 counter-cultural play, *Flash Gordon and the Angels*, appeared in London at the same time as the city's Electric Cinema was reviving the serials. In the *Guardian*, Nicholas de Jongh complained that Mairowitz had taken the myth too seriously and

Fig. 17: Flash Gordon imagery used for Wallace Berman's 'portrait of Kenneth Anger' in *Aleph*

failed to exploit its ironies, writing, 'Only William Burroughs as a pouting and slurred President [Nixon] sends the work upwards' (1971: 8).

Irony could be found elsewhere. According to Joan Hawkins, before *The Rocky Horror Picture Show* (1975) began to corner the midnight market, 'theatrical midnight screenings traditionally featured an eclectic mix of art films and trash, from *Pink Flamingos* to *Flash Gordon* serials, read ironically; that is, the audience laughed itself silly' (2000: 34). However, the arrival of *The Rocky Horror Picture Show* did not displace *Flash Gordon*. The character is referenced in the opening lines of 'Science Fiction/Double Feature', the opening song of *The Rocky Horror Picture Show*, the 1973 stage musical that became the 1975 film. In the latter the lips of Patricia Quinn and the voice of Richard O'Brien (if also often that of the cinema audience) give us: 'Michael Rennie was ill the day the earth stood still/ But he told us where we stand/ Flash Gordon was there in silver underwear./ Claude Rains was the invisible man.' *Flash Gordon* had become part of an imagined B-movie/science fiction landscape, one encompassing Universal horror films from the 1930s as well as later, relatively big-budget productions such as 20th Century-Fox's *The Day the Earth Stood Still* (1951) and MGM's *Forbidden Planet* (1956).

And the one I walked out of...: Flesh Gordon

When a feature film *Flash Gordon* was released at the end of 1980, a full page advertisement appeared in *Variety*, not advertising the just completed extravaganza, but announcing with full show business cheek: 'We have been cautioned against misleading the public with our advertisements. Do not be confused! We are the one and only... *Flesh Gordon*.' This was followed by a 'them and us' list, comparing 'their good stuff' (music by Queen) with 'Our good stuff' ('Mysterious Sex-Rays, Gay Monsters, Power Pasties, Penisauris and Rapist Robots'), 'their budget' ('multimillion dollar') with 'our budget' ('a few bucks, a lot of imagination, and a pound of killer weed') (Anon. 1980: 29).

Released in 1974, *Flesh Gordon* had appealed to the counter-cultural appropriation of Flash Gordon but more to the youth-orientated softcore sex market. Bill Landis and Michelle Clifford refer to it as 'the perennial teen make-out drive-in überhit' (2002: 42). It was a product of a particular moment when American censorship was being relaxed and the pornographic was becoming more mainstream. It was thus significant as an early porn parody but also as a relatively expensive one, with better production values than might have been expected. Howard Ziehm, who directed the film with Michael Benveniste, had a background in sex loops as well as in directing *Mona: The Virgin Nymph* (1970) and producing *Hollywood Blue* (1970), a documentary about actors who had begun their career making sex films. Originally intended as a $25,000 hardcore film, the contemporary commercial success of the sex film led *Flesh Gordon* to turn into a project with a reputed budget well over $500,000 (see Hayward 2010: 114). In turn this led to the employment of a talented special effects team and an especially composed musical score.

The 1980 'do not be confused!' tagline was in part a response to the earlier insistence that *Flesh Gordon* be clearly distinguished from its near-namesake. Thus *Flesh Gordon* opens with a printed declaration that, 'Realizing America's respect for things of the past, we in the spirit of burlesque and satire have created a new folk hero, with the spirit of the old but the outrageousness of the new.' Like the first Universal serial and the 1980 feature, its narrative begins by keeping relatively close to the Raymond comic strip, while replacing Mongo with Porno, Zarkov with Jerkoff, and Dale Arden with Dale Ardor. Its low humour and softcore sex allows it be, as Philip Hayward noted, a dual parody, of both *Flash Gordon* and of moral panics around pornography and the permissive society (2010: 115). The supposed threat from outer space is of course actually pleasurable.

The critical reception of *Flesh Gordon* was less negative than might have been expected. In Britain at least it received some relatively sympathetic reviews (as identified in the British Film Institute's Reuben Library clipping file for the film). Even Margaret Hinxman's *Daily Mail* review, which went under the heading 'And the one I walked out of...' conceded that the film had some impressive special effects. In the *Financial Times* Nigel Andrews wrote that 'the film has a cheerfulness and visual inventiveness that many more well-bred films have lacked', while David Robinson in the *Spectator* described it as 'continually smutty and sometimes obscene. It is also frequently funny.'

Hayward refers to the film's 'trash/camp aesthetic' (2010: 115) but this operates at a different level to other forms of camp and trash aesthetic explored here. Its low humour sits alongside some surprisingly elaborate stop-motion effects, including a sword fight with a skeleton and a King Kong-like one-eyed monster at the end. It acquired the reputation of existing in different versions: in *The Psychotronic Encyclopedia of Film* it is claimed that 'the original hardcore scenes have been cut a lot' (Weldon 1989: 248). That appears to be a myth. It illustrates how trash may not always be as trashy as its reputation, if also fitting Sconce's notion of sleaze in its softcore subterfuge, lurking 'at the ambiguous boundaries of acceptability in terms of taste, style, and politics' (2007a: 5–6).

Ziehm alone went on to direct *Flesh Gordon Meets the Cosmic Cheerleaders*, a delayed sequel which had less emphasis on stop-motion effects and even more on toilet humour, breasts and an obsession with virility. It retained the 1930s setting of the opening sequences, and some of the sets remained remarkably elaborate, bringing occasional steam-punk style to the relentless succession of smutty jokes. With streams of semen and singing turds, the film belongs squarely in body genre terri-tory. It was released in a different environment, amidst different bounda-ries of acceptability, and received far less attention than the first *Flesh Gordon* film.

A Camping Trip: The Flash Gordon Feature

The 1970s was otherwise the decade of unrealised *Flash Gordon* films. The most famous of these is the film George Lucas was hoping to make before he switched to *Star Wars* (1977). *Flash Gordon* was also a fondly remembered childhood experience that underlies the late 1970s transfor-mation of the American film industry, and in effect the reversal of earlier hierarchies that had tended to relegate genres such as science fiction to the B-film or the serial. The feature version that was made, directed by Mike Hodges for Dino De Laurentiis, had a troubled production, received a wide initial release, patchy box-office success (doing better in Britain than elsewhere) and complaints about its *lack* of seriousness. Greg Bear's *Los Angeles Times* article, 'Flash Gordon – A Camping Trip', encapsulated one strand of the response. In contrast to the *Flash Gordon and the Angels* review quoted above, Bear's comparison between *Star Wars* and *Flash Gordon*, at the expense of the latter, was based on a complaint against camp as 'a cruel judgement of the innocence of childhood, or the limita-tions of popular art' (1980: S78). Similarly, Peter Nichols complained that the cardinal crime of the 1980 film 'was not to take its subject matter seriously', leading to a failure to reproduce 'the innocent lunacy of its comic strip origins' (quoted in Bould 2007: 19).

The slick production values of the Hodges film means that it is out of key with most of the other films discussed here. It makes it into Rausch and Riley's *Trash Cinema: A Celebration of Overlooked Masterpieces* (2015: 89–92), but sandwiched uneasily between *Faster, Pussycat! Kill! Kill!* and *Flesh Eating Mothers* (1988). It has a trash-camp aesthetic without the relentless low humour of *Flesh Gordon*. This is evident in the garish sets, willful absurdity from the 'Flash' of the T-shirt worn by Flash Gordon (Sam Jones) and 'Flash, I love you, but we only have 14 hours to save the earth'-style dialogue, and what Mark Bould referred to as its 'polymorphously perverse' qualities (2007: 25). It is deliberate camp and trash in the sense of the excesses of its production and performance. Like the Universal serials it aimed for the look of the Raymond drawings but through brilliant colours and other forms of stylistic excess rather than the recycled black-and-white resources of the earlier films. Reviewers highlighted the way in which it worked on different levels, with Chris Peachment in *Time Out* reversing other distinctions between audiences, and looking forward to its queer appropriation, suggesting that

> adult punters will soon slip back into a reverie for the lost visions of Saturday morning cinema, and their kids can get off on the extraordinary undercurrent of febrile sexuality: strange rituals in swamps, hints of incest, impalings, plastic cat-suited women duelling with whips – a whole new index for Kraft-Ebbing. ... Flash himself is as thick as a brick, but will no doubt appeal to gentlemen who prefer blondes. (1980: 57)

It remains important to emphasise the different approaches adopted by different audiences. While the 1930s serials could be appropriated as naïve camp, or identified as more knowing than has often been assumed, those not taken with the overall lack of seriousness in the 1980 film could cling on to more reassuring values. Thus when Roy Kinnard and his co-authors looked to the feature film in their book on the *Flash Gordon* serials, they complained that it was a 'vulgar, heavy-handed put-on' but still welcomed the performances of Melody Anderson, Ornella Muti and Max von Sydow, the 'sweeping production design' and 'bright, sharp, widescreen Technicolor photography' (2005: 198).

Baytekin Fezada Çarpışanlar

Baytekin Fezada Çarpışanlar, also known as *Flash Gordon's Battle in Space*, raises other questions. It spans different cultural contexts, as a Turkish version of *Flash Gordon* but also as a 1960s Turkish film that has resurfaced on the internet, without intertitles. More specifically, *Baytekin Fezada Çarpışanlar* is a Yeşilçam (literally, green pine) film, produced by studios based on Yeşilçam Street, Beyoglu, Istanbul, in particular in the period between 1965 and 1975, when two hundred or more of such films were released annually, making the Turkish film industry one of the largest in the world (see Broughton 2013: 103). Yeşilçam films were produced quickly and cheaply, often mimicking or otherwise appropriating Hollywood genres, characters and films but also adapting them for local audiences. Thus for Iain Robert Smith (2017), Turkish films such as *Şeytan* (1974), an unauthorized version of *The Exorcist* (1973), are a testament to the pervasiveness and power of American culture but also to how that material can be transformed, revealing ways in which cultures intersect and borrow from each other. They reveal Hollywood's global reach but also local inflection. Yet the traffic has not been one way; Turkish Yeşilçam cinema, along with Hollywood remakes and variants from Latin America to the Far East, has become the subject of Anglo-American fandom since at least the publication of Pete Tombs' *Mondo Macabro: Weird & Wonderful Cinema Around the World* (1997), as local variants of Hollywood films have made their way back home.

Baytekin Fezada Çarpışanlar illustrates some of the complications within this process. The film bears some similarities to the Universal serials. Its hero leaves Earth for outer space, encounters creatures resembling the Claymen from *Flash Gordon's Trip to Mars*, and comes into contact with a villainous emperor Ming, who he eventually helps to defeat. It is different in other respects. The film starts with the dark-haired Baytekin (Hasan Demirtag) in jail. A flashback shows his return to what he insists is his birthplace and the suspicion he meets at the questions he asks. His anger at being told there are no records of him having landed him in jail, he is visited by a stranger who calls him 'The Great O' and the 'Great

Emperor', shoots the guard with a ray gun and takes him to a flying saucer (unlike the spacecraft shown in the other versions discussed here) and then to outer space.

Other *Flash Gordon* films (and even *Flesh Gordon*), begin with a succession of events closer to the initial comic strip, showing Flash, Dale Arden and Professor Zarkov (or their near namesakes) visit another planet in order to save the Earth. The change in *Baytekin Fezada Çarpışanlar* can in part be explained by the film's more immediate source material. It is an adaptation that draws not only on the Universal serials and 1950s science fiction films but also on the Turkish comic strip character Baytekin (sometimes spelt Bay Tekin). The adventures of this character first appeared in the juvenile comics *Afacan* in 1934 and *Cocuk Sesi* in 1935. According to Kaya Ozkaracalar (2009) Baytekin first appeared as Avci Bayteken, a version of Raymond's Jungle Jim, then as a version of Raymond's Secret Agent X9, and then, in 1935 in *Cocuk Sesi,* in a version of Flash Gordon. In the (very popular) Turkish comics, Baytekin did not simply exist as a Turkish version of Flash Gordon but as a character with different identities, Jungle Jim and Secret Agent X-9 as well as Flash Gordon. The Baytekin strip did in fact begin with a narrative close to that of the Raymond strip and other film versions, but in the Turkish version the character was adapted for his local audience and given his own local identity.

In drawing on this, what is immediately, if retrospectively, striking is the film's poverty of resources, even in comparison with the other films

Fig. 18: Scratched film in *Baytekin Fezada Çarpısanlar*

Fig. 19: Staging
communication
between spacecraft
in *Baytekin Fezada
Çarpısanlar*

discussed here. Ray gun fire and attacks on other spacecraft are shown by scratching on the film. The film features a number of different spacecraft but these all look remarkably similar, sharing an interior even more rudimentary than the one seen in the Universal serials, the technology getting no further than flashing lightbulbs, a blinking arrow and an assorted collection of dials and levers. Clearly the same filming locations are used to represent different diegetic locations, with little or no redressing of the sets. As in other science fiction films, the future is signified by visual as well as aural communication across space, but in *Baytekin Fezada Çarpışanlar* this illusion is created by having characters stand behind or in front of a hole in the wall. Even a television screen appears to be beyond the reach of the budget. Rather than the relative splendor of the recycled sets of the Universal serials, in this version Ming's palace is a series of cramped spaces, the sparse appearance accentuated by the extensive use of close-ups.

The film's no-budget appearance is accompanied by a disarming use of naïve science fiction imagery. A forced landing on another star lead Baytekin and his female companion to jump ship, only to be attacked by men with animal head gear and what Ed Glaser describes in his video account of the film as 'man-eating muppets' (2015). The importance of Flash Gordon's appearance and costume, from Buster Crabbe's torso and silver underwear to the T-shirt worn by Sam Jones, is here given a bizarre twist when, on board the spacecraft that takes him away from Earth, Baytekin is initially dressed in an outfit that give him a pair of

Fig. 20: Animal head gear in *Baytekin Fezada Çarpısanlar*

cone-like breasts. The gender-bending outfit is later changed for a more conventional spaceman's T-shirt, and in other respect the emphasis is on Baytekin's masculinity, if also on women as fighters and spaceship commanders. There are similarities here to an American film such as *Untamed Women*, in which male characters arrive in a land of female warriors and use the situation to teach them how to kiss. As well as emphasising his lovemaking prowess, Baytekin repeatedly insists on his fighting abilities. Warned against exploring the first star on which he lands, his response is, 'I'm not a pussy. I got two belts in my boxing league.' When arriving at Ming's palace and told, 'Our men are not that fond of women', his reply is that in Turkey men kill other men for the sake of women.

Baytekin is thus an action-man hero, but in this version without either a Zarkov or a Dale Arden, he is distinguished from other Flash Gordon portrayals in the way in which he moves from one female companion to another. By the end of the film, Baytekin has fallen in love, but to a woman who dies saving his life, leaving him to return alone to Earth. *Baytekin Fezada Çarpışanlar* constructs a more troubled version of Flash Gordon, from the man struggling to claim his own identity at the start, through the 'lost in space' man to the final, grieving figure on his way home. The film draws on the lone gunfighter of the western as much as that of Flash Gordon as innocent action hero.

A fuller understanding of this would necessitate locating the film more clearly within its industrial and cultural context, not just in terms of the material it adapts but in relation to the particular time when it was made and the structure of the Turkish film industry in the 1960s. Viewing the film as transnational trash cinema takes it away from that context and involves looking at how it has, in effect, been made psychotronic. Here even the fact that it currently circulates in a Turkish-language version without subtitles is not necessarily seen as a problem. Thus the description to the Internet Archive upload ends: 'It's in unsubtitled Turkish, but don't worry about that. Watch this if you're in the mood for something fun and crazy.' Leon Hunt's reminder that 'however deliriously out-of-this-world trash "classics" may seem, they *do* come from somewhere' (2004: 174) continues to be countered by moves to take these films away from whence they came.

Ed Glaser's Neon Harbor site provides some more context. Here *Baytekin Fezada Çarpışanlar* is remarked upon for its absurdity ('So if one time he fought puppets and changed the flow of gravity while wearing radio dials on his nipple ... well, that's just Tuesday on planet Mongo') but also as part of Turkish comic strip adaptation history. For Smith, Glaser's Deja Vue video series (where his comments on the film can be found) is an example of how looking at this material can be undertaken 'without lapsing into unthinking exoticism', or celebrating films simply for appearing 'weird and wonderful' (2017: 144, 145). Smith's own account provides a more nuanced analysis of the different forms taken by transnational adaptation, from the importance that appropriating film material had for a Turkish film production boom geared towards a local audience to the different uses of transnational adaptation in the Philippines and India.

The attention that has been paid to *Baytekin Fezada Çarpışanlar* so far has been that of the psychotronic gaze, often without particular consideration for its origins. From this perspective its inadequacies and obscurities become its appeal. 'Learn to go see the "worst" films; they are sometimes sublime', advised Ado Kyrou (2000: 71). The comment has lost some of its force on account of the number of times it has been repeated, but something sublime can be discovered in the limitations of *Baytekin Fezada Çarpışanlar*, taken away from its earlier context. Viewed in relation to other *Flash Gordon* films, it also reveals the story's adaptability, providing a further dimension to the long afterlife of apparently disposable culture.

This book started with a film first screened in 1966 and ends with one released in 1967. If this seems to keep trash cinema at a half century's distance, there are more recent examples, from the discarded VHS-aesthetic of *Trash Humpers* (2009) and the bad animation of *Birdemic: Shock and Terror* (2010) to the slick, ill-timed self-congratulation of *United Passions* (2014). However, trash cinema is also a feature of the present in the very way in which it recovers the past.

At the beginning of the twentieth century the emerging film industry could use the word 'trash' to mean the copied or the old. In the United States the Consolidated Amusement Company advertised its imported films with the announcement it sold 'ALL NEW STOCK. NO LICENSED "TRASH". NO OLD SUBJECTS' (*Motion Picture World*, May 1909, 567). Locating value in the old as well as the new has meant distinguishing between treasure and trash, rejecting much of film history in the construction of a narrative of high achievement and progress. Yet cinema has also been a story of failure, repetition and regression, the low as as well as the high. While it can seem that the mass of films have disappeared into the trash of cinema history, they are often still out there, waiting to fascinate us.

SELECT FILMOGRAPHY

The just over a hundred films listed chronologically below represent a small sample from the cinematic lowlands after the silent era. They include films that make effective or distinctive use of limited resources, films with aspirations far beyond their resources or achievement, and films that embrace a trash aesthetic. Most of the earlier films listed are American but the list as a whole aims to indicate the global nature of trash cinema.

Ingagi (William Campbell, 1930, US)
The Galloping Ghost (B. Reeves Eason, 1931, US)
Ten Minutes to Live (Oscar Micheaux, 1932, US)
Shot in the Dark (George Pearson, 1933, UK)
Maniac (Dwain Esper, 1934, US)
The Rawhide Terror (Bruce Mitchell, Jack Nelson, 1934, US)
Shadow of Chinatown (Robert F. Hill, 1936, US)
Tell Your Children/Reefer Madness (Louis Gasnier, 1936, US)
Toofani Tarzan (Homi Wadia, 1937, India)
Confessions of Boston Blackie (Edward Dmytryk, 1941, US)
Night Monster (Ford Beebe, 1942, US)
I Walked with a Zombie (Jacques Tourneur, 1943, US)
Cobra Woman (Robert Siodmak, 1944, US)
Detour (Edgar Ulmer, 1945, US)
My Name is Julia Ross (Joseph H. Lewis, 1945)
The Curse of the Wraydons (Victor M. Gover, 1946, UK)
Cat Women of the Moon (Arthur Hilton, 1953, US)
Glen or Glenda (Edward D. Wood Jr., 1953, US)

Creature with the Atom Brain (Edward L. Cahn, 1955, US)

Dementia/Daughter of Horror (John Parker, 1955, US)

The Flesh Merchant/The Wild and Wicked (Merle Connell, 1956)

Liane, das Mädchen aus dem Urwald/Liane, Jungle Goddess (Eduard von
  Borsody, 1956, Germany)

The Giant Claw (Fred F. Sears, 1957, US)

Sorority Girl (Roger Corman, 1957, US)

The Incredible Petrified World (Jerry Warren, 1959, US)

Plan 9 from Outer Space (Edward D. Wood Jr., 1959, US)

La Nava de los monstrous/Ship of Monsters (Rogelio A. González, 1960,
  Mexico)

The Beast of Yucca Flats (Coleman Francis, 1961, US)

Reptilicus (Sidney W. Pink, 1961, Denmark)

Eegah (Arch Hall Sr., 1962, US)

Invasion of the Star Creatures (Bruno VeSota, 1962, US)

Blood Feast (Hershell Gordon Lewis, 1963, US)

Flaming Creatures (Jack Smith, 1963, US)

Santo en el museo de cera/Santo in the Wax Museum (Alonso Corona
  Blake, Manuel San Fernando, 1963, Mexico)

Hercules Against the Moon Men (Giacomo Gentilomo 1964, Italy)

*The Incredibly Strange Creatures Who Stopped Living and Became Mixed
  Up Zombies!!?* (Ray Dennis Steckler, 1964, US)

The Nasty Rabbit (James Landis, 1964, US)

Wrestling Women vs. the Aztec Mummy (René Cardona, 1964, Mexico)

Bad Girls Go To Hell (Doris Wishman, 1965, US)

Il boia scarlatto/The Bloody Pit of Horror (Massimo Pupillo, 1965, Italy)

Faster, Pussycat! Kill! Kill! (Russ Meyer, 1965, US)

Scorpio Rising (Kenneth Anger, 1965, US)

Vinyl (Andy Warhol, 1965, US)

Manos: The Hands of Fate (Hal P. Warren, 1966, US)

Ôgon Batto/The Golden Bat (Hajime Satô, 1966, Japan)

The Shooting (Monte Hellman, 1966, US)

Sins of the Fleshapoids (Mike Kuchar, 1966, US)

Le spie vengono dal semifreddo/Dr Goldfoot and the Girl Bombs (Mario
  Bava, 1966, Italy)

Mars Needs Women (Larry Buchanan, 1967, US)

Marvo Movie (Jeff Keen, 1967, UK)

Shanty Tramp (Joseph P. Mawra, 1967, US)

Casus Kiran/Spy Smasher (Yilmaz Atadeniz, 1970, Turkey)

Fear Chamber (Jack Hill, Juan Ibañez, 1968, Mexico/US)

The Ghastly Ones (Andy Milligan, 1968, US)

Night of the Living Dead (George Romero, 1968, US)

A Thousand Pleasures (Michael Findlay, 1968, US)

Der Turm der verbotenen Liebe/Tower of Screaming Virgins (Franz Antel, 1968, Germany)

Angel, Angel, Down We Go (Robert Thom, 1969, US)

Fuego (Armando Bo, 1969, Argentina)

Moon Zero Two (Roy Ward Baker, 1969, UK)

La noche de Walpurgis/The Werewolf versus the Vampire Woman (León Klimovsk, 1970, Spain)

The Student Nurses (Stephanie Rothman, 1970, US)

Trash (Paul Morrissey, 1970, US)

Trog (Freddie Francis, 1970, UK)

Ginger (Don Schain, 1971, US)

Gojira tai Hedora/Godzilla vs. Hedorah (Yoshimitsu Banno, 1971, Japan)

Le frisson des vampires/The Shiver of the Vampires (Jean Rollin, 1972, France)

Private Parts (Paul Bartel, 1972, US)

Revolver (Sergio Sollima, 1973, Italy)

Les possédées du diable/Lorna the Exorcist (Jesus Franco, 1974, France)

Darna vs The Planet Women (Armando Garces, 1975, Philippines)

Female Trouble (John Waters, 1975, US)

Thundercrack! (Curt McDowell, 1975, US)

Queen Kong (Frank Agrama, 1976, UK)

A Reason to Live (George Kuchar, 1976, US)

Bad/Andy Warhol's Bad (Jed Johnson, 1977, US)

Eraserhead (David Lynch, 1977, US)

The Bees (Alfredo Zacarias, 1978, Mexico)

They Eat Scum (Nick Zedd, 1979, US)

Zombi 2 (Lucio Fulci, 1979, Italy)

The Alien Dead (Fred Olen Ray, 1980, US)

Pepi, Luci, Bom y otras chicas del montón/Pepi, Luci, Bom and Other Girls Like Mom (Pedro Almodóvar, 1980, Spain)

For Y'Ur Height Only (Eddie Nicart, 1981, Philippines)

Subway Riders (Amos Poe, 1981, US)

Vortex (Beth B, Scott B, 1982, US)

Mo/The Boxer's Omen (Chih-Hung Kuei, 1983, Hong Kong)

Ator 2: l'Invincible Orion/The Blade Master (Joe d'Amato, 1984, Italy)

Pulgasari (Sang-ok Shin, 1985, North Korea)

Thrust in Me (Richard Kern, 1985, US)

Class of Nuke 'em High (Richard W. Haines, Lloyd Kaufman, 1986, US)

Dead End Drive-In (Brian Trenchard-Smith, 1986, Australia)

Tough Ninja the Shadow Warrior (Godfrey Ho, 1986, Canada/Hong Kong)

Bad Taste (Peter Jackson, 1987, New Zealand)

Nekromantik, (Jörg Buttgereit, 1987, Germany)

Street Trash (James M. Muro, 1987, US)

Deadbeat at Dawn (Jim Van Bebber, 1988, US)

Superstar: The Karen Carpenter Story (Todd Haynes, 1988, US)

Lady Terminator (H. Tjut Djalil. 1989, Indonesia)

Things (Andrew Jordan, 1989, Canada)

Troll 2 (Claudio Fragasso, 1990, Italy)

El Mariarchi (Robert Rodriguez, 1992, US)

Showgirls (Paul Verhoeven, 1995, US)

Gummo (Harmony Korinne, 1997, US)

Freeway II: Confessions of a Trick Baby (Matthew Bright, 1999, US)

Battlefield Earth (Roger Christian, 2000, US)

The Room (Tommy Wiseau, 2003, US)

Alone in the Dark (Uwe Boll, 2005, Germany)

Angels of Destiny (Ekenna udo Igwe, 2006, Nigeria)

Kani Goalkeeper/Crab Goalkeeper (Minoru Kawasaki, 2006, Japan)

Snakes on a Train (Peter Mervis, 2006, US)

Grindhouse (Robert Rodriguez, Quentin Tarantino, Edgar Wright, Elli
    Roth, Rob Zombie, 2007, US)

Ram Gopal Varma Ki Aag/Ram Gopal Varma's Indian Flames (Ram Gopal
    Rama, 2007, India)

Birdemic: Shock and Terror (James Nguyen, 2010, US)

Pig Death Machine (Amy Davis, Jon Moritsugu, 2013, US)

Sharknado (Anthony C. Ferrante, 2013, US)

Bunny the Killer Thing (Joonas Makkonen, 2015, Finland)

The Forbidden Room (Guy Maddin, Evan Johnson, 2015, Canada)

BIBLIOGRAPHY

Anon. (1930) 'Chicagoans Fall for Serials and Mellers as Fad', *Motion Picture News*, 27 September, 45.

___ (1956) 'Review: Bride of the Monster', *Motion Picture Daily*, 7 September, 6.

___ (1958) 'Circuit Publicists at Meeting on "Macabre"', *Motion Picture Daily*, 17 July, 2.

___ (1960) '"Henry" Bows in Tonight', *Los Angeles Times*, 30 December 1960, B8.

___ (1980) 'Flesh Gordon [advertisement]', *Variety*, 17 December, 29.

___ (2012) 'So Bad So Good', *B Movie Nation*, 11 February. http://www.bmovienation.com/?p=1382 (accessed 22 April 2017).

Barefoot, G. (2017) *The Lost Jungle: Cliffhanger Action and Hollywood Serials in the 1930s and 1940s*. Exeter: University of Exeter Press.

Bear, G. (1980) '*Flash Gordon* – A Camping Trip', *Los Angeles Times*, 21 December, S78.

Beard, W. (2010) *Into the Past: The Cinema of Guy Maddin*. Toronto: University of Toronto Press.

Benjamin, W. (1999) *The Arcades Project*. Cambridge, MA: Harvard University Press.

Benshoff, H. M. (2008) 'Beyond the Valley of the Classical Hollywood Cinema: Rethinking the "Loathsome Film" of 1970', in L. Geraghty and M. Jancovich (eds) *The Shifting Definitions of Genre: Essays on Labelling Films, Television Shows and Media*. Jefferson, NC: McFarland, 92–109.

Bergan, R. (2011) 'George Kuchar Obituary', *Guardian*, 19 October.

Birchard, R. S. (1995) 'Edward D. Wood Jr. – Some Notes on a Subject for Further Research', *Film History*, 7, 450–5.

Bondanella, P. (1992) *The Cinema of Federico Fellini*. Princeton, NJ: Princeton University Press.

Bould, M. (2007) 'Oh my God, This is Really Turning Me On! Adapting *Flash Gordon*', *Film International*, 5, 2, 18–26.

Bourdieu, P. (1984) *Distinction: A Social Critique of the Judgement of Taste*. New York and London: Routledge.

Boyreau, Jacques (2002) *Trash: The Graphic Genius of Xploitation Movie Posters*. San Francisco, CA: Chronicle Books.

Brandum, D. (2016) 'Temporary Flea-Pits and Scabs' Alley: The Theatrical Dissemination of Italian Cannibal Films in Melbourne, Australia', in A. Fisher and J. Walker (eds) *Grindhouse: Cultural Exchange on 42nd Street and Beyond*. New York, NY: Bloomsbury, 53–72.

Briggs, J. B. (1989) *Joe Bob Briggs Goes to the Drive-In*. Harmondsworth: Penguin.

Broughton, L. (2013) '*Captain Swing the Fearless*: A Turkish Film Adaptation of an Italian Western Comic Strip', in L. Nagib and A. Jerslev (eds) *Impure Cinema*. London: IB Tauris, 102–18.

Bullock, M. (2012) *Memory Fragments: Visualising Difference in Australian History*. Bristol: Intellect.

Carvalho, C. (2014) 'OK, that's my fault', '*Abraham Lincoln vs. Zombie* Reviews and Ratings', Internet Movie Database, 12 September, http://www.imdb.com/title/tt2246549/reviews (accessed 27 May 2017).

Chibnall, S. (1997) 'Double Exposures: Observations on *The Flesh and Blood Show*', in D. Cartmell, H. Kaye, I. Q. Hunter and I. Wheldon (eds) *Trash Aesthetics: Popular Culture and Its Audience*. London: Pluto Press, 84–102.

Chunn, L. (1990) 'The Long and the Short of It', *Guardian*, 12 October, 46.

Church, D. (2009) 'Bark Fish Appreciation: An Introduction', in David Church (ed.), *Playing with Memories: Essays on Guy Maddin*. Winnipeg: University of Manitoba Press, 1–25.

____ (2016) *Grindhouse Nostalgia: Memory, Home Video and Exploitation Film Fandom*. Edinburgh: Edinburgh University Press.

Cline, W. C. (1994) *Serial-ly Speaking: Essays on Cliffhangers*. Jefferson, NC: McFarland.

Collins, M. A. (1997) 'Introduction', in T. Weisser, *Asian Cult Cinema*. New York, NY: Boulevard Books, 1–3.

Cook, P. (1976) 'Exploitation Films and Feminism', *Screen*, 17.2.

Craig, R. (2015) 'Manos, The Hands of Fate (1966)', in A. Rausch and R. D. Riley (eds) *Trash Cinema: A Celebration of Overlooked Masterpieces*. Albany, GA: Bear Media, 138–42.

Davies, J. (2009) *Trash: A Queer Film Classic*. Vancouver: Arsenal Pulp Press.

Davis, B. (2012) *The Battle for the Bs: 1950s Hollywood and the Rebirth of Low-Budget Cinema*. New Brunswick, NJ: Rutgers University Press.

de Jongh, N. (1971) 'Flash Gordon at the Open Space', *Guardian*, 17 February, 8.

Egan, K. (2007) *Trash or Treasure? Censorship and the Changing Meaning of the Video Nasties*. Manchester: Manchester University Press.

Farber, M. (1975) 'Blame the Audience', in T. McCarthy and C. Flynn (eds) *Kings of the Bs: Working Within the Hollywood Studio System*. New York, NY: Dutton, 44–7.

____ (1998) *Negative Space: Manny Farber on the Movies*. New York: Da Capo Press.

Fisher, A. and J. Walker (2016) 'Introduction: 42nd Street and Beyond', in A. Fisher and J. Walker (eds) *Grindhouse: Cultural Exchange on 42nd Street and Beyond*. London: Bloomsbury, 1–11.

Flynn, C. (1975) 'The Schlock/Kitsch/Hack Movies (1974)', in C. Flynn and T. McCarthy (eds) *Kings of the Bs: Working Within the Hollywood System. An Anthology of Film History and Criticism*. New York, NY: Dutton, 3–12.

Flynn, C. and T. McCarthy (eds) (1975a) *Kings of the Bs: Working Within the Hollywood System. An Anthology of Film History and Criticism*. New York, NY: Dutton.

____ (1975b) 'The Economic Imperative: Why Was the B Movie Necessary?', in C. Flynn and T. McCarthy (eds) *Kings of the Bs: Working Within the Hollywood System. An Anthology of Film History and Criticism*. New York, NY: Dutton, 13–43.

G. K. (1952) 'Fantasy, Scary Comedy Bracketed on Program', *Los Angeles Times*, 9 October, B8.

Goodsell, G. (1988) 'Corpone Angst and Green Rubber Monsters: The Films of Larry Buchanan', *Shock Xpress*, 2, 4, 30–1.

Glaser, E. (2015) 'Turkish Flash Gordon', *Neon Harbor*, posted 28 January, http://neonharbor.com/turkish-flash-gordon/ (accessed 1 May 2017).

Greenberg, C. (1939) 'The Avant-Garde and Kitsch', *Partisan Review*, 6, 5, 34–9.

Grey, R. (1995) *Nightmare of Ecstasy: The Life and Art of Edward D. Wood, Jr.* London: Faber.

Guins, R. (2005) 'Blood and Black Gloves on Shiny Discs: New Media, Old Tastes, and the Remediation of Italian Horror Films in the United States', in S. J. Schneider and T. Williams (eds) *Horror International*. Detroit, MI: Wayne State University Press, 15–32.

Hamelman, S. L. (2004) *But is it Garbage? On Rock and Trash*. Athens, GA: University of Georgia Press.

Harrow, K. (2013) *Trash: African Cinema from Below*. Bloomington, IN: Indiana University Press.

Hauser, S. (2002) 'Waste into Heritage: Remarks on Materials in the Arts, on Memories and the Museum', *Waste-Site Stories: The Recycling of Memory*. Albany, NY: State University of New York Press, 39–54.

Hawkins, J. (1999) 'Sleaze Mania, Euro-Trash, and High Art: The Place of European Art Films in American Low Culture', *Film Quarterly*, 53, 2, 14–29.

_____ (2000) *Cutting Edge: Art-Horror and the Horrific Avant-Garde*. Minneapolis, MN: University of Minnesota Press.

Hayward, P. (2010) 'Lust in Space: Science Fiction Themes and Sex Cinema', in B. Johnson (ed.) *Earogenous Zones: Sound, Sexuality and Cinema*. Oakville, CT: Equinox, 102–24.

Heffernan, K. (2007) 'Art House or *House of Exorcism*: The Changing Distribution and Reception Contexts of Mario Bava's *Lisa and the Devil*', in J. Sconce (ed.) *Sleaze Artists: Cinema at the Margins of Taste, Style and Politics*. Durham, NC: Duke University Press, 144–63.

Heuston, L. (2012) 'So Bad So Good', *Ashland Daily Tidings*, 13 February. http://www.dailytidings.com/article/20120209/ENTERTAIN/2020903 09 (accessed 9 May 2017).

Hills, M. (2007) 'Para-Para-Cinema: The *Friday the 13th* Film Series as Other to Trash and Legitimate Film Cultures', in J. Sconce (ed.) *Sleaze Artists: Cinema at the Margins of Taste, Style, and Politics*. Durham, NC: Duke University Press, 219–39.

Hitchens, G. (1964) 'The Truth, the Whole Truth and Nothing but the Truth about Exploitation Films, *Film Comment*, 3, 2, 1–13.

Hoberman, J. (1991) 'Bad Movies', in *Vulgar Modernism: Writings on Movies and Other Media*. Philadelphia, PA: Temple University Press, 13–22.

Hoberman, J. and J. Rosenbaum (1991) *Midnight Movies*. New York, NY: Da Capo.

Hogrefe, J. (1984) 'The "Euros" Take Manhattan', *Washington* Post, 22 July, K1.

Holliday, R. and T. Potts (2012) *Kitsch!: Cultural Politics and Taste*. Manchester: Manchester University Press.

Hollows, J. (2003) 'The Masculinity of Cult', in M. Jancovich, A. Lazaro-Reboll, J. Stringer and A. Willis (eds) *Defining Cult Movies: The Cultural Politics of Oppositional Taste*. Manchester: Manchester University Press, 35–53.

Hooton, C. (2016) 'Enjoyment of Trash Films Linked to High Intelligence, Study Finds', *Independent*, http://www.independent.co.uk/arts-entertainment/films/news/enjoyment-of-trash-films-linked-to-high-intelligence-study-finds-a7171436.html (accessed 23 April 2017).

Hunt, L. (2004) 'Burning Oil and Baby Oil: *The Bloody Pit of Horror*', in E. Mathijs and X. Mendix (eds) *Alternative Europe: Eurotrash and Exploitation Cinema Since 1945*. London: Wallflower Press, 172–80.

Hunter, I. Q. (2013) *British Trash Cinema*. London: BFI/Palgrave Macmillan.

_____ (2014) 'Trash Horror and the Cult of the Bad Film', in H. M. Benshoff (ed.) *A Companion to the Horror Film*. Chichester: Wiley, 483–500.

_____ (2015) 'The Road to Excess', *Sight & Sound*, 25, 9, 32–3.

Hunter, I. Q. and H. Kaye (1997) 'Introduction – Trash Aesthetics: Popular Culture and its Audience', in D. Cartmell, H. Kaye, I. Q. Hunter and I. Wheldon (eds) *Trash Aesthetics: Popular Culture and its Audience*. London: Pluto Press, 1–13.

Jacobs, L. (1992) 'The B Film and the Problem of Cultural Distinction', *Screen*, 33, 1, 1–13.

James, N. (2007) 'Welcome to the Grindhouse', *Sight & Sound*, 17, 6, 16–18.

James, S. E. (2012) 'Adorno', in C. A. Zimring and W. L. Rathje (eds) *Encylopedia of the Consumption of Waste: The Social Science of Garbage*. Los Angeles, CA: Sage, 4–5.

Jancovich, M. (2002) 'Cult Fictions, Cult Movies, Subcultural Capital and the Production of Cultural Distinctions', *Cultural Studies*, 16, 2, 206–22.

_____ (2012) 'Relocating Lewton: Cultural Distinctions, Critical Reception, and the Val Lewton Horror Films', *Journal of Film and Video*, 64, 3, 21–37.

Jmajors3 (2007) 'these are the greatest actors who ever lived', '*Transmorphers* Reviews and Ratings', Internet Movie Database, 26 June, http://www.imdb.com/title/tt0960835/reviews?ref_=tt_urv (accessed 27 May 2017).

Juzwiak, R. (2015) 'NYFF: Guy Maddin and Evan Johnson Talk Indulgence, Trash, Poppers, and Celine Dion', *Defamer*, 10 January, http://defamer.gawker.com/nyff-guy-maddin-and-evan-johnson-talk-indulgence-tras-1734041416 (accessed 27 May 2017).

Kael, P. (1970) 'Trash, Art and the Movies', in *Going Steady: Film Writings 1968–1969*. London: Marion Boyars, 87–129.

____ (1997) 'The Current Cinema: Mothers', in A. R. Pratt (ed.) *The Critical Response to Andy Warhol*. Westport, CT: Greenwood Press, 90–4.

Kerekes, D. (1986) 'Letter', *Shock Xpress*, 4, 6.

Kerr, P. (1983) 'My Name is Joseph H. Lewis', *Screen*, 24, 4–5, 48–67.

Kinnard, R., T. Crnkovich and R.J. Vitone (2005) *The Flash Gordon Serials, 1936-1940*. Jefferson and London: McFarland.

Kitses, J. (1996) *Gun Crazy*. London: British Film Institute.

Kleinhans, C. (1993) 'Taking Out the Trash: Camp and the Politics of Irony', in M. Mayer (ed.) *The Politics and Poetics of Camp*. New York, NY: Routledge, 182–201.

Kyrou, A. (2000 [1963]) 'The Marvellous is Popular', in P. Hammond (ed.) *The Shadow & Its Shadow: Surrealist Writing on the Cinema*, 3rd edition. San Francisco, CA: City Lights Books, 68–71.

Landis, B. and M. Clifford (2002) *Sleazoid Express: A Mind-Twisting Tour Through the Grindhouse Cinema of Times Square!* New York, NY: Fireside.

Lázaro-Reboll, A. (2016) 'Making Zines: Re-Reading *European Trash Cinema* (1988–98)', *Film Studies*, 15, 30–53.

'Ledster' (2014) 'European Trash Cinema', 8 April 2014, https://europeantrashcinema.blogspot.co.uk/2014/04/welcome-to-blog-about-trashy-side-of.html (accessed 9 July 2017).

Lucas, T. (2015) 'Total Trash', *Sight & Sound*, 25, 9, 26–31.

MacDonald, D. (1962) 'Masscult and Midcult', in D. MacDonald, *Against the American Grain*. London: Victor Gollantz, 3–75.

Maltby, R. (1995) 'The Production Code and the Hays Office', in T. Balio (ed.) *Grand Design: Hollywood as a Modern Business Enterprise, 1930–1939*. Berkeley, CA: University of California Press, 37–72.

Margulies, E. and S. Rebello (1983) *Bad Movies We Love*. New York, NY: Plume.

Martinez, J. M. (2016) 'When Bad Means Good: The Bad Film Society', *Rogue Valley Messenger*, 28 July, http://www.roguevalleymessenger.com/when-bad-means-good-the-bad-film-society/ (accessed 9 May 2017).

Mathijs, E. (2005) 'Bad Reputations: The Reception of "Trash" Cinema', *Screen*, 46, 4, 451–72.

_____ (2011) 'Exploitation Cinema', in K. Gabbard (ed.) 'Oxford Bibliographies Online: Film and Media'. Oxford and New York: Oxford University Press.

Mathijs, E. and X. Mendix (eds) (2004) *Alternative Europe: Eurotrash and Exploitation Cinema Since 1945*. London: Wallflower Press.

Mathijs, E. and J. Sexton (2011) *Cult Cinema: An Introduction*. Chichester: Wiley-Blackwell.

Mayer, J. P. (1946) *Sociology of Film: Studies and Documents*. London: Faber.

Medved, H., and M. Medved (1980) *The Golden Turkey Awards: Nominees and Winners, the Worst Achievements in Hollywood History*. New York, NY: Puttnam.

Medved, H., M. Medved and R. Dreyfuss (1978) *The Fifty Worst Movies of All Time (And How They Got That Way)*. London: Angus & Robertson.

Mekas, J. (2016) *Movie Journal: The Rise of the New American Cinema, 1959–71*. New York, NY: Columbia University Press.

Metz, W. (2003) 'John Waters Goes to Hollywood: A Poststructural Authorship Study', in D. A. Gerstner and J. Staiger (eds) *Authorship and Film*. New York, NY: Routledge, 157–74.

Mikelbank, P. (1993) 'Haute Gauche: The Trash Master', *Washington Post*, 17 July, F1.

Morgan, K. (2017) 'Spellbound', *Sight & Sound*, 27, 4, 40–4.

Morton, J. (1986) 'Educational Films', in V. Vale and A. Juno (eds) *Incredibly Strange Films*. London: Plexus, 166–8.

Olney, I. (2013) *Euro Horror: Classic European Horror Cinema in Contemporary American Culture*. Bloomington, IN: Indiana University Press.

Ozkaracalar, K. (2009) 'Debut of Flash Gordon in Turkey', *The*

Mysterious Flame of Queen Lona. http://kayaozkaracalar.blogspot.co.uk/2009/10/debut-of-flash-gordon-in-turkey.html (accessed 28 April 2017).

Palmer, R. (2006) *Hershell Gordon Lewis, Godfather of Gore: The Films.* Jefferson, NC: McFarland.

Peachment, C. (1980) "Flash Gordon [review]', *Time Out*, 12–18 December, 57.

Peary, D. (1982) *Cult Movies: The Classics, the Sleepers, the Weird and the Wonderful.* London: Vermillion.

Pitts, M. R. (1997) *Poverty Row Studios, 1929–1940.* Jefferson NC: McFarland.

Potamkin, H. (1933) 'The Ritual of the Movies', *Nation Board of Review Magazine*, 8, 5, 3–6.

Potts, R. (2007) 'The New B Movie', *New York Times*, 7 October, E18.

Rausch, A. and R. D. Riley (eds) (2015). *Trash Cinema: A Celebration of Overlooked Masterpieces.* Albany, GA: Bear Media.

Rayns, Tony (2016), 'The Forbidden Room', *Sight & Sound*, 26, 1, 68–9.

Read, J. (2003) 'The Cult of Masculinity: From Fan-Boys to Academic Bad Boys', in M. Jancovich, A. Lazaro-Reboll, J. Stringer and A. Willis (eds) *Defining Cult Movies: The Cultural Politics of Oppositional Taste.* Manchester: Manchester University Press, 54–70.

Ridley, J. (2010) 'Christian Scare Films: The Unlikely Pairing of Director Ron Ormond and Preacher Estus Pirkle', in R. Weiner and J. Cline (eds) *Cinema Inferno: Celluloid Explosions from the Cultural Margins.* Lanham, MD: Scarecrow Press, 229–35.

Rosenbaum, J. (2016 [1994]) 'The Way We Weren't', https://jonathanrosenbaum.net/2016/12/the-way-we-weren-t/ (accessed 23 April 2017).

Ross, A. (1989) *No Respect: Intellectuals and Popular Culture.* New York, NY: Routledge.

Rotha, P. (1934) 'Queen Christina', *Cinema Quarterly*, 2, 3, 185–6.

Sanjek, D. (2000 [1990]) 'Fans' Notes: The Horror Film Fanzine', in K. Gelder (ed.) *The Horror Reader.* London: Routledge, 314–25.

Sarkhost, K. and W. Menninghaus (2016) 'Enjoying Trash Films: Underlying Features, Viewing Stances, and Experiential Response Dimensions', *Poetics* 57, 40-54.

Sarne, M. (1970) 'Movie Mailbag: Who's Right about *Performance*?', *New*

York Times, 20 September, 14.

Sarris, A. (1961-62) 'Notes on the Auteur Theory in 1962', *Film Culture*, 27, 35-51.

_____ (1975) 'Beatitudes of B Pictures', in C. Flynn and T. McCarthy (eds) *Kings of the Bs: Working Within the Hollywood System. An Anthology of Film History and Criticism*. New York, NY: Dutton, 48–53.

Schaefer, E. (1999) *Bold! Daring! Shocking! True! A History of Exploitation Films, 1919–1959*. Durham, NC: Duke University Press.

_____ (2012) 'Adults Only: Low-Budget Exploitation', in C. Lucia, R. Grundmann and A. Simon (eds) *Wiley-Blackwell History of American Film*. Oxford: Wiley-Blackwell, 291–308.

Schumark, M. (1960) 'Nudity Features in Film "Quickies"', *New York Times*, 15 June, 51.

Schwartz, C. (1996) *Videohound's Guide to Cult Flicks and Trash Pics*. Detroit, MI: Visible Ink.

Sconce, J. (1995) '"Trashing" the Academy: Taste, Excess, and an Emerging Politics of Cinematic Style', *Screen*, 36, 371–93.

_____ (2003) 'Esper, the Renunciator: Teaching "Bad" Movies to Good Students', in M. Jancovich, A. Lazaro-Reboll, J. Stringer and A. Willis (eds) *Defining Cult Movies: The Cultural Politics of Oppositional Taste*. Manchester: Manchester University Press, 14–34.

_____ (2007a) 'Introduction', in J. Sconce (ed.) *Sleaze Artists: Cinema at the Margins of Taste, Style, and Politics*. Durham, NC: Duke University Press, 1–16.

_____ (2007b) 'Movies: A Century of Failure', in J. Sconce (ed.) *Sleaze Artists: Cinema at the Margins of Taste, Style, and Politics*. Durham, NC: Duke University Press, 273–309.

Segrave, K. (1992) *Drive-In Theaters: A History Since Their Inception in 1933*. Jefferson, NC: McFarland.

Shaviro, S. (2002). 'Fire and Ice: The Films of Guy Maddin', in W. Beard and J. White (eds) *North of Everything: English-Canadian Cinema Since 1980*. Edmonton: University of Alberta Press, 216–21.

Sherman, B. (2009) 'Interview: Bobcat Goldthwaite', *Boston Phoenix*, 1 September, http://thephoenix.com/boston/movies/89022-interview-bobcat-goldthwait/ (accessed 7 May 2017).

Sim, J. (1988–89) 'Hollywood in the Bronx: George Kuchar's Perverse Comedies', *Shock Xpress*, 2, 5, 36.

Simon, J. (1970) 'The Most Loathsome Film of All?' *New York Times*, 23 August, D1, 5.

Simon, R. K. (1999) *Trash Culture: Popular Culture and the Great Tradition*. Berkeley, CA: University of California Press.

Sitney, P. A. (1990) 'The Cinematic Gaze of Joseph Cornell', in K. McSchine (ed.) *Joseph Cornell*. New York, NY: Museum of Modern Art, 69–89.

Smith, I. R. (2017). *The Hollywood Meme: Transnational Adaptation in World Cinema*. Edinburgh: Edinburgh University Press.

Smith, J. (1997 [1962–63]) 'The Perfect Filmic Appositeness of Maria Montez', in J. Hoberman and E. Leffingwell (eds) *Wait for Me at the Bottom of the Pool: The Writings of Jack Smith*. New York, NY: High Risk Books.

Smith, P. (2016). '"This is Where We Came In?": The Economics of Unruly Audiences, Their Cinemas and Tastes, From Serial Houses to Grind Houses', in A. Fisher and J. Walker (eds) *Grindhouse: Cultural Exchange on 42nd Street and Beyond*. London: Bloomsbury, 31–51.

Snelson, T. and M. Jancovich (2011) '"No Hits, No Runs, Just Terrors": Exhibition, Cultural Distinctions and Cult Audiences at the Rialto Cinema in the 1930s and 1940s', in R. Maltby, D. Biltereyst and P. Meers (eds) *Explorations in New Cinema History: Approaches and Case Studies*. Chichester: Wiley-Blackwell, 199–211.

Solover, B. (2012) 'Our Sincere Thanks', 'Manos on HD', http://www.manosinhd.com/our-sincere-thanks/ 5 August (accessed 8 May 2017).

____ (2015) 'The Press Release', 'Manos on HD', http://www.manosinhd.com/our-sincere-thanks/ 21 August (accessed 8 May 2017).

Sontag, S. (1983 [1964]) 'Notes on Camp', *A Susan Sontag Reader*. Harmondsworth: Penguin, 105–19.

Stam, R. (1997) 'From Hybridity to the Aesthetics of Garbage', *Social Identities: Journal for the Study of Race, Nation and Culture*, 3, 2, 275–90.

Stanfield, P. (2011) 'Going Underground with Manny Farber and Jonas Mekas: New York's Subterranean Film Culture in the 1950s and 1960', in R. Maltby, D. Biltereyst and P. Meers (eds) *Explorations in New Cinema History: Approaches and Case Studies*. Chichester: Wiley-Blackwell, 212–25.

Stelter, B. (2013) 'Sharks Tear Up Twitter, If Not the TV Ratings', *New York Times*, 13 July, C3.

Stevenson, J. (1989), 'Letter', *Shock Xpress*, 3, 1, 3.

_____ (2003) *Land of a Thousand Balconies: Discoveries and Confessions of a B-Movie Archaeologist*. London: Headpress.

Szpunar, J. (2013) *Xerox Ferox: The Wild World of the Horror Fanzine*. London: Headpress.

Taves, B. (1995) 'The B Film: Hollywood's Other Half', in T. Balio (ed.) *Grand Design: Hollywood as a Modern Business Enterprise, 1930–1939*. Berkeley, CA: University of California Press, 313–50.

Taylor, J. R. (1976–77) 'Beyond the Taste Barrier', *Sight & Sound*, 46, 1, 37–9.

Thompson, D. (2002) 'Auteur of Darkness', *Sight & Sound*, 12, 8, 16–18.

Thompson, M. (1979) *Rubbish Theory: The Creation and Destruction of Value*. Oxford: Oxford University Press.

Thornton, S. (1996). *Club Cultures: Music, Media and Subcultural Capital*. Cambridge: Polity.

Tinkcom, M. (2002) *Working Like a Homosexual: Camp, Capital, Cinema*. Durham, NC: Duke University Press.

Tohill, C. and P. Tombs (1995) *Immoral Tales: European Sex and Horror Movies 1956–1984*. New York, NY: St Martin's Griffin.

Tombs, P. (1997) *Mondo Macabro: Weird & Wonderful Cinema Around the World*. London: Titan.

Tooze, G. (2017) *'Multiple Maniacs* [Blu-ray]', *DVD Beaver*, http://www.dvdbeaver.com/film6/blu-ray_reviews_75/multiple_maniacs_blu-ray.htm (accessed 5 May 2017).

Tzioumakis, Y. (2006) *American Independent Cinema: An Introduction*. Edinburgh: Edinburgh University Press.

Vale, V. and A. Juno (1986) 'Introduction', in V. Vale and A. Juno (eds), *Incredibly Strange Films*. London: Plexus, 4-6.

Vincendeau, G. (2017) 'Against', *Sight & Sound*, 27, 4, 33.

Warner, S. (2014) 'The Banality of Degradation: Andy Warhol, the Velvet Underground and the Trash Aesthetic', in S. Whiteley and J. Sklower (eds) *Counter-Cultures and Popular Music*. Farnham: Ashgate, 45–60.

Waters, J. (1986) *Crackpot: The Obsessions of John Waters*. London: Macmillan.

_____ (1991 [1981]) *Shock Value: A Tasteful Book about Bad Taste*. London: Fourth Estate.

Watson, P. (1997) 'There's No Accounting For Taste: Exploitation Cinema and the Limits of Film Theory', in D. Cartmell, H. Kaye, I. Q. Hunter and I. Wheldon (eds) *Trash Aesthetics: Popular Culture and Its Audience.* London: Pluto Press, 66–83.

Weiner, R. G. (2010) 'The Price of Exploitation: Dwain Esper', in J. Cline and R. G. Weiner (eds) *From the Arthouse to the Grindhouse: Highbrow & Lowbrow Transgressions in Cinema's First Century.* Lanham, MD: Scarecrow Press, 41–51.

Weldon, M. (1989) *The Psychotronic Encylopedia of Film.* London: Plexus.

Whiteley, G. (2011) *Junk: Art and the Politics of Trash.* London: IB Tauris.

Williams, L. (1991) 'Film Bodies: Gender, Genre and Excess', *Film Quarterly,* 44, 4, 2–13.

Zimring, C. A. (2012) 'Introduction', in C. A. Zimring and W. L. Rathje (eds) *Encyclopaedia of the Consumption of Waste: The Social Science of Garbage.* Los Angeles, CA: Sage, xxv–xxvii.

INDEX